A

LOST
SHEPHERD

An Ex–Priest's Journey *from* Sin *to* Salvation

Michael E. Ripple

Other titles available from New Hope Press

Are The Medjugorje Apparitions Authentic?
Wayne Weible and Dr. Mark Miravalle

The Medjugorje Fasting Book
Wayne Weible

Medjugorje: The Message (CD Audiobook)
Wayne Weible

A Message of Peace (DVD)
Original publisher: Boston Center For Peace

A

LOST
SHEPHERD

An Ex–Priest's Journey *from* Sin *to* Salvation

Michael E. Ripple

New Hope Press
Hiawassee, Georgia

Library of Congress Control Number: 2 0 1 2 9 3 2 3 1 9

ISBN: 978-0-9820407-3-7

June 2012 First Printing

Published by New Hope Press
Hiawassee, GA 30546
www.newhopepresspub.com
newhopepress@windstream.net

Photograph, Front Cover: Wendy Ripple M.D.
Jacket Design: Janice Walker
Editorial Assistance: Marsha Blasco

Printed in the United States of America

Dedicated to the Blessed Virgin Mary,

Kraljica Mira.

ACKNOWLEDGEMENTS

To Wendy, my lovely wife—whose love, patience, proofreading and prayers (which I am sure were grammatically correct) sustained me through many a day and year.

To Isaac, my son—for years of childlike inspiration, wonderment, laughter and love.

To my father, 'Pappy'—for unending encouragement, and keeping me in supply of a computer, an attorney and late night coffees.

To the remarkable friends I met along the way and between the pages. Especially to Beverly—not only for inviting me into the quest of memoir, but also for teaching me the art of truth in story.

To Wayne—for wisdom, guidance and now a friendship with both he and his wife, Judi.

Lastly, to the priests, bishops, and individuals who are part of this story, both the living and dead—may the living know true peace and may the dead rest in the presence of Christ.

God bless you.

FORWORD

Michael Ripple's manuscript arrived at our office in early 2011. Betty Cooper, assistant publisher for New Hope Press, put it on my desk and left a note on the cover page stating, "You really need to read this one…"

Upon seeing the title of the manuscript, *A Lost Shepherd: An Ex–Priest's Journey from Sin to Salvation*, I immediately went to Betty and said, "There is no way we are going to publish a book about an ex–priest!" I handed it back to her, adding, "Once a priest—always a priest!"

Betty remained resolute: "Listen; just read it…what do you have to lose?"

Reluctantly, I began to read Michael Ripple's story, a saga of prodigal return, which to my surprise, involved the intercession of the Blessed Virgin Mary through her unprecedented 31–year–plus run of daily apparitions at the little village of Medjugorje. I could not stop reading the manuscript; the story stoked the full range of my emotions, the key element necessary in any good book to make it worthwhile to read. I read the manuscript a second time, now beginning to understand why Betty had been so persistent.

The very human story shows the grace of conversion rising from the innocent quest of a young boy to become a Roman Catholic priest and live his life in service to his God; and, to be one with Him. When boyish goals turn into age of reason doubts, grace begins to fade and reality sets in. The war for his soul is on. It is a roller coaster ride filled with moments of triumphant goodness and painful failure. There is little in between the two.

Michael's story is a raw exposure of the constant skirmish between the desire to be and do good, and the humanity that dwells within each one of us. It is unique in that this is the battle of a soul convinced that he is to be a Roman Catholic priest. The forces of darkness are determined to prevent it. We see the same struggles in Michael's quest that impound all of us in our own attempts to live a faith–based life.

What makes the story of a lost shepherd intriguing is the fact that this is a person committed from a young age to the holy profession of priesthood. We do not normally think of someone who has a call to the religious life as having to struggle with it. We do not think of priestly vocations going through the same doubts and failures as do the faithful. However, I can attest from my 26 years of involvement in spreading the message of Medjugorje, that I have never met a priest—and I have met hundreds of them through my mission—who has not had crisis in his vocation.

Michael's story turned out to be a revelation for me; yes, I still believe a priest is a priest forever. However, just as in our own daily lives, there are exceptions. The story highlights the forgiveness and compassion of God, even for those who fail not just in a religious vocation—but any vocation or calling.

Anyone who seeks God knows He does not give up on a soul until the last moment of life. We may not fulfill our life mission as we originally intended; we may have to resort to plan B or C or higher. Eventually though, if we sincerely attempt to follow goodness as best we can, we will accomplish what we are placed on earth to do. Michael has done that up to this point in his life. He is now "high priest" to his wonderful family of wife Wendy and son Isaac.

This book is an instrument of help for those individuals attempting to determine a call to vocation—and possibly even a call to those who have left the Catholic faith to return. It allows the laity an intimate peek at the struggle that takes place when a soul commits to being a servant of God. More importantly, we understand why the Blessed Virgin Mary, as the messenger of Medjugorje, constantly asks us to pray for the shepherds of the Church.

Such a journey is never going to be smooth and easy. However, with the example of Michael's story, perhaps it will make it a little easier for others to discern, accept, survive and triumph in their service to God.

—Wayne Weible

On *the* Outside

2005

"Therefore, you shepherds, hear the word of the Lord."
—from the prophet Ezekiel.

CHAPTER I

I didn't know I was looking for answers.
I didn't know I had questions.
I thought I had it all...

Halfway across the world in a church much too small for the mass of humanity gathered there, I tried to kneel in adoration of the Holy Eucharist as people pressed in on all sides. It was impossible to move.

I stretched to catch a glimpse of the Blessed Sacrament beyond the throng of pilgrims filling the packed church. A cloud of smoke floated above the altar creating a display of shadows and light as the incense burned and its scent filled the air. If only the incense could mask the smell of body odor, I thought.

An old woman with a brown babushka and arthritic knuckles leaned against me. She thumbed her worn rosary beads and her lips moved in silent prayer. More people were pushing in through the huge front doors. Each person who entered set off a chain reaction that looked like grains of sand slowly shifting positions. I was jostled several steps against my will until it was impossible to hold my place. In a few moments, I was involuntarily maneuvered out of the side door by the will of the crowd.

I put my hands in the pockets of my worn khaki blazer and felt for my rosary beads as I meandered along the walkway worn smooth by the feet of millions of religious pilgrims.

Just as well, I thought. I don't really belong here. Taking a deep deliberate breath, I slowly exhaled and muttered, "I wouldn't have been able to pray in that crowd anyway."

Outside, the cool spring air awoke me from my incense–induced stupor. I walked by the entrance and looked at the clock on the bell tower. It was a little past 10 o'clock on a weeknight and the church was packed for Eucharistic Adoration. I walked to the front of the carved wooden doors propped open, and once more caught a glimpse of the altar and the gold monstrance, where the round piece of unleavened bread, the presence of the Body of Christ, was safely displayed. The Host now appeared to be glowing red as if it were on fire.

I glanced at all the people, hundreds of them gazing and praying, and grew envious of their passion. Unlike them, I felt no strong emotion, positive or negative. We were all sharing a pilgrimage on a warm April night in the year 2005.

From distant places around the globe, as so many before us, we had traveled here to pray in the small village of Medjugorje, located deep in the mountains of Bosnia–Herzegovina. The village was now an internationally famous religious destination, where the Blessed Virgin Mary, the mother of Jesus Christ, first appeared to six Croatian children in June 1981. She was still regularly appearing to three of the original six youths who were now well–known visionaries.

I knew from the books I read before coming on pilgrimage that the apparitions taking place in little Medjugorje were the lon-gest–lasting daily Marian apparitions in the history of the Roman Catholic Church. The theme of the Virgin's messages was simple: Get back to God.

I had no idea that message was meant for me.

In spite of the area's early Communist persecutions, a devas-tating civil war and doubting Croatian bishops, the Mother of God was continuing to lead her children back to the heart of her Son, Jesus. From all religions, millions of people, millions of seekers and millions of sinners were offering prayers in this place. I was now one of them; but tonight, there was no room for me. It doesn't matter; I thought with sadness, I really don't even know how to pray anymore.

I made my way to a wooden bench on the side of the church, took a seat and leaned back. Behind me were more benches and a row of outdoor confessionals that reminded me of a small 10–room motel; little cards by the doors indicated the language each priest could accommodate. I now understood why some called Med-jugorje the "Confessional for the World."

For the moment though, no one was in line and no priests were present to hear confessions. It was just me sitting between the church and the confessionals, thumbing the rosary and crucifix in my jacket pocket.

"Jesu Christo," spoke a deep, slow guttural voice over the loud speaker coming from the service being held inside Saint James Church.

"Jesu Christo," I repeated aloud as I stood and walked by a statue that resembled a dwarf Franciscan friar.

"Jesu Christo," the voice said again.

A sacred silence seemed to surround the area. I felt the urge to kneel down alone in the open, dark space. The sound of an engine broke the silence. Headlights appeared and an old rusty Fiat ran up over the curb and onto the paved stone walkway. The car passed within a few feet of me, screeching to a halt. The passenger doors quickly opened and two Franciscan friars jumped out, left the doors ajar and ran up the steps leading to the back sacristy door, their white rope cinctures dangling behind them. They knocked hard and somewhat frantically on the door with the loud thumps sending echoes into the darkness.

The driver stayed in the car and revved the engine, which continued to putter out a smoky, noxious exhaust. The back sacristy door opened and a crack of light escaped into the night. The silhouette of the friar inside made a deliberate sign of the cross as the other two shared some seemingly urgent news. With the message apparently delivered, the friars ran back down the steps and returned to the car. The driver did a tight U–turn and the car sped off as quickly as it had come.

Over the loudspeaker, a voice spoke another prayer, first in Croatian, then in English: "In thanksgiving for the life and death of our Holy Father."

The driver's urgency and the friar's panic now made sense. "He died;" I whispered softly, "Pope John Paul has died."

I closed my eyes and remembered him.

I had received the Sacrament of Confirmation the same day John Paul II was elected pope. We had his papal blessing for the Ripple family framed and hanging in our home and I had a prayer card with the picture of his face on it as a young John Paul.

I had shared the priesthood of Christ with Pope John Paul. I was ordained a Roman Catholic priest under his papacy. The same hands that broke the bread and poured the wine, the same hands that healed and blessed the sick, the same hands laid upon the disciples ordaining them to go forth and proclaim the kingdom of God; those same hands—Jesus' hands—that were placed upon John Paul, were placed upon me.

Tonight a brother priest had died.

Outside of the church alone in the dark, I knelt, bending over until my face was inches from the ground. I had left the Church that ordained me, after being a priest and having my eyes opened to the darker realities of the priesthood as well as myself. I left after realizing I would never fit the model of the parish priest, and after becoming angry at an institution that no longer had room for me or my new life; I left after being excommunicated.

I knelt there, outside the Body of Christ and I felt empty.

I felt like a lost shepherd.

From a place deep within my soul, a prayer began to form. It passed through my lips as a verbal whisper into the darkness: "John

Paul—pray for me, a priest ordained under you; now lost, sinful and forgotten."

Pray for me...
Pray for my wife...
Pray for our son.

the Quest

1965–1992

"It was not you who chose me, but I who chose you..."
—from the Gospel of Jesus Christ according to John.

CHAPTER II

Standing at the bathroom sink washing my hands, I turned the water off and glanced in the mirror, barely tall enough to see my whole face. I smiled and whispered, "This is the best day of my life!"

I was seven years old.

Having just returned home from my first Holy Communion, there was no immediate desire to be with family, have cake or open cards. All was overshadowed by a yearning to go back into the church and stare at the giant crucifix behind the altar and the gold tabernacle. When I was there, I felt like I could talk directly to God and I wanted more of Him; I wanted to be alone with God.

The next thought that popped into my mind was *I should become a priest*. That was it—no booming thunder, no fireworks or flashes of light going off; just a sink, a mirror and a little boy with an excited heart.

That moment is the beginning of my story.

I arrived late into the family, an unexpected addition, when my brother George was 12 and my sister Claudia, 14. Before my birth, everything seemed settled in my family. Mom had taken a new night–shift nursing position at nearby District General Hospital after assuring the nun that she was done having children. Dad was the manager at the local Sherwin Williams Paint Store.

Two incomes, two kids—life was good. In fact, George was hoping for a canary rather than a baby brother. Six years later, George and Claudia were gone and I was alone with my parents.

Every Sunday Mom, Dad and I would attend Mass at our home parish, Saint Mary's Catholic Church. It was one of the largest parishes in Maryland. There were eight Masses each weekend with two of them occurring in the parish social hall. I was raised liturgically on folding chairs without kneelers, portable altars and guitars. We always sat in the last row on little wooden chairs.

Every Sunday, I stared at the backs of people's coats and dresses and never saw what was going on way up front on the portable wheeled altar. When it came time for Communion, Mom would go up to receive while Dad, a Methodist, stayed with me. Sometimes Dad went to his church and then we would all meet for doughnuts at the parish cafeteria.

When I was eight years old, I became an altar boy and the first Mass I served was on Mother's Day. During the summer, the public school kids always served the 6:45 A.M. daily Mass. On the days when I was scheduled to serve, I rode my new brown Schwinn bicycle from our neighborhood down the hills into town and through the brick–paved alleys to St. Mary's massive building. Usually, I would hop off the bike and lock it to the downspout at the back sacristy door.

I would enter the church hoping it was still dark inside and that I was alone. I loved an empty church and enjoyed feeling as if I had God's undivided attention. Whenever the red sanctuary candle was burning, I knew Jesus was there. He was somehow in the Host within the gold tabernacle behind the altar. I never doubted He was there. In my heart, I talked to Him as I got ready to serve at the altar for Mass.

I would put on my black cassock and white pleated surplice, light the candles and pour the water and wine into the two glass cruets the priest would use to pour into his chalice. I would set the chalice on a table next to the altar and place the little gold plate, or paten, on top of it.

A prayer was taped to one of the sacristy cupboards, encouraging the priest to celebrate the Mass as if it were his first, his only and his last. I whispered the prayer with an awe and reverence that came from a place known only to my soul. I felt like God was always with me. Even more, I felt like God wanted me. God's presence was a perfectly natural daily occurrence, an occurrence that I really could not explain to anyone.

During the fall and winter months, the parish held Monday evening devotions, a mixture of Eucharistic Adoration, the Rosary and Benediction. I loved it when I was scheduled as the altar boy for these special evenings.

Monsignor James Murphy, or "Murph" as he became known to me, who had a particularly strong devotion to the Blessed Mother, would lead the weekly prayers. The Monday evening devotions were his creation. Murph was half–blind and his hearing matched his sight. He was in his 80's, and because there were four other younger priests, Murph celebrated only one Mass each weekend.

Monsignor Murphy showed such care and attention when he carried the Host to the monstrance on the altar. After he closed the little gold door on the cross–shaped monstrance, he held onto the corner of the altar and walked to the front where I would be kneeling. I would stand and hold the censer out for him and watch intently as he placed two little spoons of incense on the charcoal. Clouds of smoke would rise and the smell of incense would fill my nose and soak into my boyish soul. I always knelt next to him and thumbed my rosary beads, quite sure that one day I would be just like him—a priest; maybe even one with the honorary title of Monsignor.

Monsignor Murphy noticed my new bike one day following the Mass. He surprised me and came outside with a little book and a plastic bottle of holy water. "Michael, you need to have your bike blessed," he said.

The elderly priest held the book close to his good eye and thumbed the pages to find a blessing. There we stood, just outside the back door to the church at seven in the morning. To me, this was all in a day's work of being a priest. It was natural. He smiled at me, shut the book, tapped me on top of my head and said, "Be safe, son."

St. Mary's was a good place for a kid. From youth group events to street fairs, there was always something to do. My parish even put some money in my pocket during the high school summers; in addition to my own painting and contracting work, I picked up extra hours doing maintenance on the buildings or in the parish cemetery.

Priests came and went through the years at St. Mary's, but Monsignor Murphy was never transferred. He was too old. At 16, I became his chauffeur, driving him around in his rusted 1976 silver Chrysler New Yorker. As I would turn the key to start the ignition, like clockwork he would say, "Mary, Queen of the Highways, protect us." He then began the rosary and if we finished it before our final destination, he would start another one.

Monsignor Murphy never asked me if I wanted to be a priest. Instead he would say, "Michael, pray to the Virgin. She will lead you to her Son."

He must have known something.

CHAPTER III

It was Holy Thursday, the Triduum, the beginning of the three high holy days of the Catholic calendar. I was home on spring break from my first year of college formation at Saint Xavier Seminary. I stood in front of the mirror in the sacristy of St. Mary's, and adjusted the white tab collar in my black robed cassock.

I had entered Saint Xavier Seminary directly from high school, putting me on an eight–year track to becoming a parish priest. It was the natural progression in my desire to be with God and to be totally united with Him. The journey was long; not only did I have four years of college ahead of me, but also four years of graduate seminary after college.

As I looked in the mirror, I felt sick to my stomach. Something was wrong. Everything I had come to believe in wanting to pursue and become a priest seemed to be falling away. I stared at myself in the mirror, with my long, grown–out permed hair and dark shaded glasses, all packaged in a new cassock and white collar—dressed like some pretend priest. I looked the part, but I didn't feel it. I simply wasn't sure of just who I was or what I really wanted after these few months in seminary.

I knew one thing for certain—I had to quit seminary.

There were two reasons: The first was a girl; the second, a guy.

The girl was Angela, my high school sweetheart. She and I had gone to our senior prom as friends and ended up falling in love. She was my first steady girlfriend and even though she knew my plans to become a priest, it never was an issue since it would be eight years before I would be ordained. We spent countless summer evenings together, all the while growing more and more in love.

By the end of the summer, a part of me second–guessed my decision to go to seminary. That was the beginning of my doubts about becoming a priest. It was too late to apply to another college and I certainly didn't want to skip a year. In addition, Mom was starting to act a bit strange. She either really wanted me to become a priest or she simply didn't want me to be with Angela. It took much energy to keep the peace and to assure her, even with my doubts that I wasn't going to change my plans.

Further complicating matters, Angela urged me to pursue my plan so I wouldn't have regrets later. I began seminary knowing that I had to trust what I believed for the past couple of years. But, my heart was tugged in the opposite direction by love for Angela.

Every student was assigned to a priest as his spiritual director. Father Tom Britmann was assigned to me. It was very difficult to connect with him on any level. He was always talking about how each person's personality affected their spiritual development and practices. When I shared how my feelings for Angela were affecting my desire to become a priest he answered, "Did you take it to prayer?"

At that time and age I had no idea exactly what that meant. Instead of learning how to discern my call to priesthood, I was introduced to some sort of psychological approach to spirituality. I was on my own to devise my spiritual practices, which usually amounted to falling asleep while praying the rosary.

None of the other guys in seminary had girlfriends that I knew of, leaving me alone in my quandary. I decided that if I were meant to be with Angela, then God would let me know by the end of the year. However, if I were to become a priest, then He eventually would take away my feelings for Angela.

I operated and existed on spiritual naiveté. The months and miles apart only made our adolescent hearts beat stronger for each other.

Now, I stood in front of the mirror, not yet 20, but already a young man with a divided heart.

The guy—the second and more troubling reason I felt I needed to leave the seminary—was another seminarian. Just a few weeks prior and late at night, he made unwanted sexual advances towards me. I was able to remain calm and get myself out of the situation, but by the time I got into the hallway, I was in complete shock. I made my way to the community restroom, went into a stall and had dry heaves.

Walking through the seminary property and buildings that night, I felt angry, resentful and confused. How could I have allowed myself to be put in such a predicament? Eventually outside in the courtyard I found the grotto and poured everything out to the Virgin Mary.

Following that episode, most of my nights were spent sneaking into the main chapel and sleeping in a side alcove just in sight of the tabernacle. I was careful to awake in time and shower before morning prayers. My thought was if I put myself physically next to Jesus, I would be able to make sense of what had happened. Not only was I embarrassed by the advances, it opened my previously sheltered eyes. I began to look at everyone differently and almost overnight, realized I trusted no one.

I started trying to determine which seminarians were gay, and to also wonder about the priests I knew. Just before Easter break I finally found the nerve to approach my spiritual director and tell him what happened and how angry and confused I was.

"Look, Michael, these things happen when men live together," he told me. "That's just the way it is."

That was it? I thought. I just had a major thing happen to me and all I get is 'That's just the way it is?'

After wanting to become a priest for as long as I could remember, I wasn't able to make sense of what Father Tom had told me. It seemed a whole subculture existed in the church and I never had a clue. Was being gay just accepted? How could that be? "That's just the way it is," I repeated, now even more confused.

I fixed my cassock and walked out of the sacristy. At that moment, I didn't know if I could accept the new reality of seminary and priesthood and I wondered if I would ever wear a priest's collar. Perhaps the whole experience was God's way of telling me that I didn't fit in.

My two problems were too big to ignore. One month later, I left the seminary.

I stayed enrolled at the university, and took career tests through the guidance department, trying to focus on my academics so I could graduate with a marketable degree. The assessment tests revealed that I ought to consider some form of religious life or ministry—great, I thought.

Everyone in my family was fine with my decision to leave, except Mom. She took it hard and it seemed as if she was making my life miserable in hopes that I would reconsider. It made me wonder if my potential priesthood was more about her than Jesus or me.

I decided to move out of the house for the summer and live with my brother George. The happiest person was Angela, which made for a great summer. Mom and I were able to reconcile before I left for my second year of college. The few priest friends I had continued to stay in touch with were supportive of my decision.

Old Monsignor Murphy said it well one Sunday while I cleaned up the sacristy following Mass: "Michael, God still loves you. Just pray to Mary to help you."

I felt relieved, and I even felt close to God again.

CHAPTER IV

During my last year at St. John University, I was a resident advisor in the boys' dormitory. One evening after making the final rounds for the night, and after making sure all the girls were out, the doors locked, and the hallways clear of drunken freshman, I got back to my room and crashed on my bunk. The howling wind jostled my windows just enough to keep me from falling asleep. Finally, I picked up the rosary my mother had made me and began to slowly thumb the beads and meditate on the five Sorrowful Mysteries. I quietly thought about the first mystery, 'The Agony in the Garden,' then prayed an Our Father, followed by 10 Hail Mary's and a Glory Be.

When I began the third decade, 'The Crowning of Thorns,' I suddenly felt sharp jagged pricks covering my head. It felt as if someone had filled a knit cap with briars and then quickly pulled it down tight over my ears. I moved my head slightly from side to side, up and down, testing and feeling, wondering if it was a pinched nerve. The pain pierced directly into the middle of my head.

I stood up and walked around the room. Nothing helped. The pain did not subside for hours.

I woke up the next day pain free but with no understanding of what had happened to me. The winter storm had virtually shut down the campus and the town. I had to go somewhere to sit and think about what happened the night before.

I bundled up and walked off campus to St. Paul's Church. It was like hiking in the Arctic. I walked on the road since the sidewalks were nonexistent, hidden in the snow. During my three-block walk, only one car passed by, its tires packing the snow with a squeak. I passed a homeless man who wore three coats and a Pittsburgh Steelers cap. I watched as he rummaged through the trash at McDonald's, found a newspaper and stuffed it into his jacket. He then followed me into the church.

Once in St. Paul's, I made my way to the front of the church and sat in a pew while blowing into my cold, cupped hands. The steam radiators clanged, knocked, hissed and echoed throughout the empty church. The darkness and chill inside was only trumped by the unrelenting wintery blasts of the east coast storm going on outside. I shivered, pulled my jacket up around my neck, and stared at the flickering vigil light burning by the tabernacle. Just like when I was an altar boy so many years ago, I was in my favorite place. As always, it was only Jesus and me and today, a homeless man.

I always visited this place when I needed peace or time to think. This was where I came when I began to realize that my feelings for Angela were changing. It was a surprise to her when I suggested we break up and it was just as confusing to me because I had no one else I wanted to be with. I just knew and felt that I needed to be alone and I needed to be honest with Angela. This was also the place I came when I couldn't decide whether to pursue law or teaching, and when I simply needed a break from working in the dorm. Now I needed to be here because I couldn't shake a spiritual gnawing. Even though I had left St. Xavier and minor seminary and had a great three years of college life at St. John's, the feeling of wanting to become a priest never fully left me.

Everything and every moment in my life seemed to point me in the direction of returning to seminary and pursuing priesthood. Eventually I was able to make more sense of what had happened three years ago at St. Xavier. It was just a bad mix and a bad time. The diocese replaced the seminary administration soon after I had left, which I interpreted as the Church trying to improve minor seminary and make it a healthier environment.

More importantly, I felt ready to embrace the practice of celibacy, which I once thought might be difficult. I dated a few times after Angela, but felt no real desire for a relationship. I accepted it as God's signal that I would be able to live as a celibate. There was no doubt that I was attracted to women; but, I believed if I became a priest, God would help me remain loyal and celibate.

Above all else, I wanted to be with God; I wanted to be a disciple of Christ and I wanted to become a priest. If I had had a time machine, I would have traveled back in time to be one of the Apostles, to be united totally with Christ. Perhaps the world would judge this as abnormal; perhaps even the Church would. However, I believed the only way for me to unite my soul with Christ was to become a priest and to offer His Body and His Blood to the world.

I glanced over at the crucifix and noticed the crown on Christ's head. I wondered if the events of last night had really been God calling to me.

Again, I knew what I wanted to do, and a renewed sense of peace filled my heart.

CHAPTER V

My family and friends were not surprised at my decision to return to seminary. They seemed to know me better than I knew myself.

I set a box of books in the hallway just outside my room at Saint Francis Seminary. "Whew...it's a hot one," I said to my brother. He pushed past me carrying an armful of clothes on hangers. I pulled the bottom of my T–shirt up to wipe the sweat from my forehead.

"You want them in the closet?" he asked.

George was never one to engage in what he deemed as unnecessary conversation. He had always been that way. For the longest time I thought he simply didn't like me. Over the years, I began to realize he was just very utilitarian when it came to conversation. Eventually, I learned to adapt to his style. "Yeah, that's fine. Thanks."

George hung up the clothes then walked over to the open window and rested on the windowsill, hoping to catch a late summer breeze. I stood in the middle of the room and looked around. I was at St. Francis Seminary in Chambersburg, Pennsylvania. My residence hall had been built in the traditional monastic architecture with old oak doors, transepts and 12–foot high ceilings. Outside my window stretched a panorama of old and new buildings, farmland and mountains. The monastery residence was directly across an alley, just below my window. It looked like an eight–story honeycomb, with each monastic cell having its own narrow window.

I took a deep breath. The smell of new paint and carpet was tempered by the strong aroma of antiquity, a scent only noticed in a building pushing 100 years of age. I felt as if I had stepped into history, and was experiencing the past and the future all at the same time.

There was an old worn desk, a wooden chair and a brown–painted bookcase aligned against one wall. In the corner was a green vinyl chair with metal arms and legs, and duct tape on the cushion. Beside it stood a new table that served as a lampstand, magazine–rack and end table. I looked around and realized this would be my space for prayer and study for the next five years. It was going to be my little cave, where I would meet my God and spend all my waking moments getting ready to be His priest.

Mom walked into the room with Dad. She held a blue bucket, a sponge, a chamois, and a bottle of Turtle Wax. "Here, this is a little gift for you," she said with a slight smile as she handed it to me.

"Wow, thanks, guys," I said, happy because it wasn't something religious. Our eyes met and I felt her love.

"Now where are your sheets and bedspread? I'll make your bed."

I appreciated the offer, but also felt embarrassed. "Mom...no, really, I can do it."

"Here they are," Dad said, as he flopped a green garbage bag onto the mattress.

George stood and fanned his shirt. "Come on, let's go. What else do we need to unpack?"

By evening, Mom, Dad and George had done all they could; they walked to their cars to begin the three–hour trip home. I blew another kiss to Mom. Their black Chrysler New Yorker headed down the driveway and onto the narrow two–lane road that passed in front of the massive, gothic red–brick St. Francis Basilica. George followed behind in his Ford pick–up. He honked his horn and gave me a thumbs up as he drove away.

I walked over to the basilica, passing in front of a statue of St. Francis of Assisi. After a moment of hesitation, I turned and walked through one of the structure's giant heavy wooden doors. It smelled like a mixture of pork and sauerkraut. From the aromas in the air, I imagined that the friars had finished evening prayers and were cooking in their refectory.

I walked down a back circular stairway and entered the crypt beneath the nave of the church. Just ahead of me was a stone grotto. A statue of the Virgin Mary and a smaller statue of a little girl kneeling in prayer were set on ledges hewn into the rock and made to look like a cave. The odor of wax and incense was strong.

I walked into the small room, sat in one of the four pews and whispered some Hail Mary's.

On my way back to my room, I looked for the seminary chapel. From the hallway, the entrance looked like nothing more than a door to an ordinary room except for a fancy piece of cut glass. I turned the tarnished and wobbly brass knob, and entered and looked for the holy water to bless myself, but couldn't find a font anywhere.

In fact, there were no statues, no stations on the walls nor candles nor votive lights in the small room. There was only one devotional: a tabernacle situated in a tiny alcove, illuminated by a spotlight above. I suspected the sparse approach must have been the monastic influence. The Blessed Sacrament, the Body of Christ, was reserved in a small metal box on a wooden shelf. The only color in the room came from two stained glass windows, one of St. Francis; the other his contemporary, St. Clare. Twenty wooden desk chairs were arranged in front of the wooden altar. In the corner was an upright piano. I was drawn to the simplicity of it all.

If only life in seminary was as simple as the chapel décor.

CHAPTER VI

Despite all that had happened thus far, I entered St. Francis with the same romanticized vision of priesthood; one that hearkened back to my formative years at St. Mary's with Monsignor Murphy. There were about 20 seminarians living in St Anthony Hall. We lived, prayed and studied together. We were considered 'diocesan,' which meant we would complete our studies and then leave to serve as a priest in a specific diocese. There were also Franciscans who took classes with us, but did not live with us. Their rooms were in the monastery residence, and they ate and prayed with their Franciscan brethren, a group of about 80.

Perhaps I would have been better able to adjust to seminary if I had a more substantial faith foundation. In truth, I was the product of a Church that seemed to be looking for a new identity. I arrived at seminary as the last of the Baby Boomers and the first of Generation X. I was taught very little in parish religious education outside the basics for sacramental preparation. Teaching the tenets of the Faith was replaced with simplified emotional appeals. "How does that make you feel?" was the tagline.

I knew God made me, but never knew why. In all my years, I was never taught the difference between mortal and venial sin. When I arrived at the seminary, I was like a sponge, ready and willing not only to pursue a deeper relationship with Christ, but also to seek knowledge of the Faith and traditions.

Perhaps my expectations were too much.

The seminary rector was on sabbatical when I arrived. He returned and continued to work through his own spiritual dilemmas, sometimes right in front of the student body. Authority was left wanting.

So were academics. I had no idea what was right and what was wrong. We were in an age when academic freedom was being pushed past the limits of the Church Magisterium, the teaching body of the Roman Catholic Church. Again, I didn't know if this was the norm for major seminaries. Early on, I had some instructors who played with theologies that were not condoned by Rome. Not knowing any better, I accepted independent thinking and academic scholarship as a harmless pursuit of the truth. Since authority was absent, I really had no academic guidelines.

I also learned during my first year that the seminary offered little in the way of devotional practice. Aside from two or three seminarians who would pray the rosary in the Lourdes Grotto down in the crypt of the basilica, there were no other communal devotions. Twice a day, Monday through Friday, we would gather in the small chapel; first for Morning Prayer, and later for Evening Prayer and celebration of the Mass. For the most part, we were on our own for Saturday and Sunday worship. We never had Eucharistic Adoration or even Stations of the Cross during Lent. To be honest, I made no effort to change this.

For my year–end evaluation, Father Hank, the vocation director from my diocese, met with me in one of the empty guest rooms in St. Anthony Hall and gave me my summer assignment as a Boy Scout chaplain. I could not believe the irony of my life! Years ago, I had been kicked out of the Cub Scouts for fighting with the den mother's son.

Thus, after nine months of learning about the Church's need to become more relevant and culturally sensitive, I lived in the woods for two months. I became a wanna–be–hippy and a tree–hugger—and a vegetarian. In addition, even though I was the Catholic chaplain, I could not mention Jesus Christ for fear of offending someone. I had to be politically correct and ecumenically sensitive to the detriment of my own faith.

One lazy summer day, a diocesan priest arrived to visit the troop from his parish. I was looking forward to having Mass. I asked him if he wanted me to schedule it and get the word out. His answer was a yes and a no; he wanted to have Mass, but not with his troop of scouts—only with me.

There we stood, two men in the middle of the woods. One of us dressed in priestly garb celebrating Mass, and the other dressed in a Boy Scout uniform complete with shorts and green knee socks. The priest even preached to me. It was corny and freaky, and I vowed that day never to become that kind of a priest.

At the end of my summer assignment, I packed my bicycle for a four–day trek; my destination would be the Grotto of Lourdes in

Emmitsburg, Maryland, not too far from where I grew up. It was identical to the grotto in the crypt at St. Francis, and was a replica of the actual shrine in Lourdes, France, where in 1858, St. Bernadette had a vision of the Blessed Virgin Mary.

The grotto in Emmitsburg was built on the mountain where Saint Elizabeth Ann Seton lived. St. Elizabeth, who began her ministry to the people and the children of the area as a wealthy Anglican widow, converted to the Roman Catholic Faith and founded a community of religious sisters who lived a life of common prayer and service. My mother had a relic from St. Elizabeth, a tiny fragment of her body in a little round glass case. As a child, I would look at it for hours wondering from what part of her body it had come.

It was my first pilgrimage and I loved it.

I pedaled in silence for four days and made all the spiritual connections of the soul's journey. I slowly climbed hills and coasted on the flats. On August 15, the Feast of the Assumption of the Blessed Virgin Mary, I parked my bike at the base of the giant gold statue of Mary, walked to the grotto and said a Hail Mary. I stood there still not knowing why I felt called to ride to this place. I just felt I had to do it.

I returned to St. Francis a few weeks later to continue my pursuit of God and begin my next year of study.

After the little bicycle "pilgrimage", I was sure I was in the right place and doing the right thing.

CHAPTER VII

The whole sky was aglow with the purples, pinks, and oranges of the early morning sunrise. I sat on the steps of the huge, porcelain–tiled porch of St. Anthony Hall. It was punctuated with ornate cement arches and banisters. The first rays of the morning sun began peeking over the crevices and the valleys of the mountains. I smiled, remembering how I had scaled those hills on my bike trip a few months earlier. The aroma of coffee from my cup mixed with the smells of autumn leaves.

The entire scene looked like it had been recreated from Eden. I was Adam in the garden and God was strolling nearby. Stillness surrounded me and I felt His presence. I let my imagination soar and slowly sipped the coffee to enjoy the moment of grace. Something was missing, though. I wanted more God. I was restless and wanted some kind of a spiritual adventure.

For the next couple of months, I faithfully rose before sunrise and sat in the dark chapel before the Blessed Sacrament. At night, I fell asleep hugging a crucifix or praying the rosary. I was falling in love with God even more and I couldn't get enough.

Then, just as I was celebrating my success, just as I was sure I was finally moving in the right direction in my pursuit of God, I stopped. Not only did I stop—I did a spiritual 180.

Her name was Catherine, and she was married.

Catherine had short blonde hair, hazel eyes, a cute smile and a raspy voice. I had known her since high school. She was the cheerleader and friend who would always help me get suited as the school mascot. One evening, I ran into Catherine and her husband at the mall. I was thrilled to meet someone from back home and feel reconnected. As the months progressed, I learned too much about her life. Cathy wasn't as happily married as I originally imagined. One day, she said to me, "You know, Michael, I always thought you'd ask me out back in high school."

"I guess it's too late now," I joked. She didn't laugh.

There I was; instead of entering deeper into prayer and seeking union with Christ, I stayed up at night thinking about a woman; and once again, second-guessing my vocation. Maybe I just wanted to love and to be loved. Maybe I was projecting all my desires for union with God into a relationship with a woman like Catherine. I didn't know how to sort through the feelings.

I met with my spiritual director weekly. Some days the meetings brought great clarity and purpose to my continued quest for union with Christ. On other days, I fell into despair, not because I couldn't be with Catherine, but because I wondered if God wanted me as much as I wanted Him.

A few months passed and I found no peace. In desperation, I arranged to stay at a nearby Trappist monastery in Virginia in the dead of winter, arriving at the door of the monastery determined to discern my relationships. I felt that I needed to pray my way through this.

I lost track of how many days I had been on retreat, when I was paid a visit. I had just made the two–mile hike from the guest-house to the monastery chapel for midday prayer and was warming myself in the pew. I wasn't thinking or praying about anything or anybody.

A man sitting in the pew behind me leaned forward and whispered in my ear, "You have no idea how much I love you."

I turned around. No one was there.

I shook my head and wondered if I had imagined the voice. No, not only did I hear the voice, I felt it. It brought such peace and excitement—God told me he loved me!

I was sure I had heard it and wished Cathy would hear something in her heart that would free me. If only she would say: "I'm over you."

During the summer, I worked at a spirituality and psychology institute for priests at Seton Hall University. I spent the long days of summer driving speakers to and from the airports, attending lectures and eating daily meals with the spiritual giants of the time: Basil Pennington, a Trappist monk, and Benedict Groeschel, a Franciscan who was in the midst of beginning a new religious Franciscan community. They were men who felt called to go deeper into prayer and service to the poor and they wanted to recapture the spirit of St. Francis, who gave up everything and became a beggar for Christ. I was jealous of their spiritual zeal and ability to leave everything to serve.

Sometimes I hopped a train to the Bronx where I'd make a Holy Hour with these dedicated servants of God and have dinner with them. My summer was filled with reading, and I was introduced to the lives of the saints and spiritual classics. I read *Dark Night* poetry by St. John of the Cross, and St. Augustine's *Confessions*. I spent some evenings sitting in the campus chapel reading my little paperback edition of *The Cloud of Unknowing*. I would read a chapter, close my eyes and practice praying.

It was a good summer. I was inspired by holy men of a Holy Church. I deliberately stayed out of Cathy's issues with her marriage, while going deeper with my God.

It all happened just in time.

CHAPTER VIII

It was the day after Thanksgiving. We were eating turkey and mayonnaise sandwiches, warmed–over stuffing, cold home-made cranberry sauce and leftover sweet potatoes. Dad and George were in the basement of our home playing the pinball machine and watching football with my sister Claudia, her husband, Kirk, and my nephew and niece, Matt and Beth.

The kitchen upstairs was empty except for a sink load of dishes and Mom. I heard the dishes clanking in the kitchen sink and decided to go help. I knew something was bothering her.

"Mom, what's wrong?" She didn't say a word. She didn't even turn from the sink to acknowledge me. She just gave a slight cough.

From behind, I noticed the roots of Mom's short dark hair were showing their true gray. Her hands worked the dishrag furiously, one that she had knitted. She always said that they lasted forever. She tilted her head back, used her bifocals to check a plate, and then pushed the rag and the plate back into the sudsy water.

Mom leaned forward, coughed, and rested her elbows on the sides of the sink. The sleeves of her sweater were pushed up, revealing her olive skin and the strong arms of a German farm girl from over half a century ago. She rinsed the plate and placed it in the strainer, all the while ignoring me. "Mom, come on."

She coughed again and continued washing. I reached out and took her left arm. The strength of my grip revealed my frustration. "Please," I said, squeezing harder for attention, "Come on, Mom, what's wrong?" She turned and looked at me. Her bottom lip quivered. Mom had thin lips that curved downward, almost pouty; her smile was always in her eyes, one green and one brown. She glanced down at my hand on her arm.

"I'm, I'm sorry," I said, realizing what I'd done. "I didn't mean...." She coughed and turned back towards the sink. I surmised that she was upset with my sister. Every time Claudia would visit with her family, she and Mom always had some conflict. I gave up long ago, trying to figure it out, just as I gave up now.

I made the 100–mile drive back to the seminary late Sunday evening, and was in my room when a knock came at my door. It was one of my instructors, Father Derek, who usually kept to himself. It was a rare occurrence for him to be walking the halls, especially this late.

"Mike, can you come to my office?"

Now what, I thought, why can't he just tell me what he needs right here? Derek was such a control freak. He had me walk 100 yards down the hall to sit in his office. I never hit it off with him and this didn't help our relationship. He was one of my teachers during my first year of seminary. I had received a 90 percent on my first exam in his class. As the semester wore on, my scores kept going down until by the final I was in the 50 percent range.

One day while having lunch in the seminary dining room, I opened my mail and pulled out the corrected blue book. My exams were so heavily marked in red that the auxiliary bishop of my diocese noticed the corrections from the seat next to me. The bishop eyed the blood–red ink covering the pages of my essays with words like 'Heresy!' and 'No!' written in the margins of almost every page.

I shook my head in disbelief and said, "Crap. Would you look at that? Oh, sorry Bishop, I didn't mean for anyone to hear me."

The bishop laughed. "Perhaps you should buy your professor a new pen. He seems to have used quite a bit of ink on your exam."

My mind returned to the dark hallway as I obediently followed Derek to his office. His white cincture swished side to side with each purposeful step. I attempted to make some conversation. "So, how was your Thanksgiving, Father?"

"It was nice."

I gave up. I did not want to play the game. Instead, I figured I ought to conserve my energy in order to stay focused on whatever issue he had with me.

Once in his office, I discovered the pressing concern that had to be discussed so late at night. He was upset with me because the people I had entered as candidates for our class academic representatives no longer attended seminary and had left more than a year ago. I was found guilty of making a mockery of academia.

That was one way to look at it. There was also some truth and humor in what I had done. Academic representatives had no say in our academics; it was a yearlong lame–duck position. In humor, I nominated people who had long since left the program. What did it matter if they were there or not? I felt established enough to use some humor to send a message, and, in all honesty, part of me enjoyed seeing him frustrated.

The next day, I returned to my room after my last afternoon class. A red light was blinking on my answering machine. It was Dad, and the number he left for me was for the hospital. "Dad, what's wrong?"

His voice was nervous, "The doctor admitted Mom for some tests because of that cough she's had. She's down getting some x–rays right now."

Mom stayed at the hospital for another 30 days. She was diagnosed with ovarian cancer. Her chest cavity filled with fluid because of the tumor and the cancerous fluid pressed on her lungs and made her cough.

Mom was a praying mom. She prayed at all places and at all times. She silently prayed during long car rides, thunderstorms and always in bed. Sometimes from my bedroom at night, I'd hear her rosary beads fall and hit the old oak sideboard of the bed on the way to the floor. They were the greenish glow–in–the–dark beads. I used to cup them in my little hands and charge them under the lamp on the nightstand, I then hurried and crawled under the covers—their cool, green glow lit up the little crucifix.

Mom prayed during the evening news when pictures of the war in Vietnam were flashed on our black and white television. My brother George was somewhere on an aircraft carrier. She prayed every time Notre Dame University or the Pittsburgh Steelers played football. She prayed every night when my sister left to begin her new life away from our home. When my Mom was in her teens, she brought home the papers to join the Sisters of Mercy and her older sister tore them up. Therefore, instead of becoming a nun, she became a mom and taught me how to pray.

Despite all of Mom's prayers and our prayers, the cancer came and made its home in her.

It was the day after I was installed into the ministry of Acolyte, another step on the way to ordination, when I realized that Mom would not get better. The installation ceremony was not grand or formal. Usually the parents and families of the young men came to the seminary for the evening and a visiting bishop did the honors. Mom and Dad couldn't make it.

Less than 24 hours after being made an acolyte, I took Holy Communion home for Mom. She lay in bed and looked up at me with tears in her eyes. I opened the little round golden pyx container that held the Body of Christ, picked up the Host and said officially for the first time, "This is the Lamb of God, who takes away the sins of the world. Happy are those called to receive Him."

Mom replied weakly, "Lord I am not worthy to receive you, but only say the word, and I shall be healed."

Mom soon fell asleep, and I went into my bedroom, closed my eyes and stared at suffering and death.

CHAPTER IX

For the next year I lived somewhere between the seminary, a summer parish assignment and home. During this time, and just a few months before I was to become a deacon, Mom's cancer progressed with a vengeance. She was quickly dying. I had to adapt my schedule to help at home in the evenings, and then head back to the seminary or the parish in the mornings.

It was a confusing and draining time—physically, spiritually, and emotionally. I was living a vigil, but for what? Was it for ordination or death?

One morning as I was walking to my Christology lecture, I saw the professor step into the hall, look directly at me and then shut the door. A few seconds later, I opened the door and proceeded to my seat.

"Mike?"

I continued to my seat. Yes, my name is Michael. You've known me for four years. Why all of a sudden are you wondering if it's me?

"Mike—your hat."

Of course, I hadn't deliberately worn it into the classroom to annoy him. "Yes, sorry Father," I said, giving the churlish school-boy reply. Then, he was happy. I tossed the hat towards an empty chair next to my seat. It spun a perfect circle and landed softly.

"Cool," my classmate said. He leaned over and whispered, "That was a perfect toss!"

I sat and fumed for the rest of the class. Mom was dying. I was alone. Seminary was lousy.

Back in my room, I called Cathy. "Michael, is something wrong?"

"Yeah, everything."

In a whisper she said, "Hey, I'm going up to Scranton to visit Joyce. Do you remember her? Why don't you come along? It's just for a couple of days. It will do you good."

What did I have to lose? "Yeah, why not."

"Great, I'll meet you in the parking lot at eight."

I parked my T–Bird in the lot, put in a cassette tape and waited. Soon I recognized the headlights of Cathy's car. She pulled up the little hill leading to the front of the basilica. I caught her smiling as she backed in next to me. Cathy reached in the backseat and pulled out an overnight bag. I could feel my heart beating faster.

I knew what I was about to do could go one of two ways. Either it would be what we planned, an innocent getaway for me to deal with Mom's impending death and the absurdities of the seminary; or, it would be an excuse for us to play with our passions. I mumbled to myself, "God be with me," as Cathy got in the car.

We headed east and I joked about us driving to Atlantic City and playing the slots so she and Dave could put money down on a house. There was an awkward silence. I broke it by asking, "What did you tell him?" I had to know what her husband thought about us going on a road trip together.

"He knows you, Michael. He's known you since grade school. He knows you're like a brother to me. Why?—you getting weird on me or what?"

Maybe I was getting weird. The wrongness of the situation hit me again. Here I was taking off on a road trip with a married woman. Even more troubling, I did have feelings for her. Part of me hoped she still wanted me, while the other part hoped she didn't.

I sat in silence trying to analyze the situation. She had suggested I go on the trip with her. So, she must not feel attracted, I reasoned. If she was no longer attracted to me, then this was nothing more than a chance to get away from the seminary and cancer. That thought made it easier for the moment.

"What about you? Did you tell anyone you were leaving?" she asked.

"Yeah, John knows, and I told Dad I was taking off for a day or two."

John was a priest and my best friend at St. Francis. He knew everything about me, and I about him. He worked as a mechanic at the monastery garage, where I would on occasion skip class and hang out.

The T–Bird cruised along the road through the mountains of Pennsylvania. The Susquehanna River traveled with us from time to time, sometimes near the edge of the roadway, rewarding our attention with a spectacle of glistening moonlight.

Then it happened: Thump! Thump! Thump!

"What was that?" Cathy asked.

"I don't know."

Thump! Thump! Thump!

"What?"

"Something's wrong with the wheel."

"Is it a flat?"

"No, but something is definitely screwed up."

I pulled off the highway and onto a gravel–strewn parking lot. I grabbed a flashlight from the trunk, knelt down by the driver's front wheel and tried to peer behind it. Cathy followed me and stood nearby.

"I don't believe it!" I yelled, slapping my palms against the tire.

I looked in disbelief at the brake caliper. Instead of being located in its usual position pressing against the brake pads, it was now dangling behind the wheel. It was easy to see I had lost one of the front brakes. "We can't drive on this."

I stood up and our eyes met. Cathy looked as dejected as I felt. I walked to the back of the car and put the flashlight back in the trunk. When I turned, she was standing next to me, trying to make eye contact. I avoided looking directly at her. "We better head back. I'll get you a room on the seminary guest floor and you can head out tomorrow to Joyce's place."

Cathy pressed herself closer and leaned into me. Oh, Lord, no, I thought, I can't do this, but I can't keep myself from wanting her. I moved away and headed to the driver's seat.

Back in the car, she turned to me and said, "Look, it's late. Let's just find somewhere to stay. Tomorrow you can either call for a tow or drive back."

I rested my chin on the steering wheel and stared blankly at the dark highway ahead of us. I could smell her perfume. She leaned across the console of the car, looked at me and said, "I want to spend one night with you Michael, that's all—just one night."

My heart raced and my mind couldn't catch up. I blankly stared into the darkness. It's midnight, I thought, and I'm in the middle of nowhere, in a car that has lost one brake, with a married woman who wants to be with me.

I didn't have the energy to get myself out of the predicament I helped to create. Besides, for that moment, it felt good to feel wanted, even if it was sinful.

I lay next to her on the bed in the hotel room, pushing the limits and playing with the fire of our unmet physical desires. Eventually we both fell asleep, without making any physical commitment. I got up, pulled a chair by the window and sat there in the dark, pouting and daring God to notice me.

I justified it. It was all about me. I didn't care about Cathy's problems with her marriage. People deal with dying parents all the time and people live with unmet expectations and unrealized dreams all the time. I sat and wallowed in self–pity. I acknowledged lust, and added mental adultery to my examination of conscience. I topped it off with pride.

Jesus teaches us that a soul can't serve two masters. It will hate one and love the other, or be devoted to one and despise the other. I fell in and out of sleep knowing I had chosen to be mastered by my physical desires, even if they were unfulfilled. I had failed as a friend and as one aspiring to a life of celibacy.

In the morning, I found Cathy in the bathroom crying. We sat on the edge of the bed in the motel room in awkward silence, both staring at the heavy drapes that kept out all the light. During the drive back to St. Francis we started to explain it away. I was lonely; so was she; I had pressures; and, so did she. We both used each other and it was wrong. We spoke the words, and maybe even believed and understood them, but it didn't erase the guilt and shame.

Once back at the seminary, Cathy took off for Scranton. I drove down to the garage where I knew John would be and pulled the car right into the stall with the lift. He was leaning against the tool bench holding an oil filter in a rag. He looked to me like Jesus is often portrayed, with his long hair and beard and deep set eyes that always looked straight through you.

"Do you know what that thing is?" I joked.

"Ripple!" he hollered. "You came back! Everything okay?" He moved over to the workbench, grabbed a Styrofoam cup tattooed with grease and took a sip of coffee. "Where were you? You look like crap."

I looked at my watch. I had already missed morning prayers and breakfast; my first class was about to begin. "The caliper came off the T–Bird last night."

We put the car on the lift and the hydraulics hummed as the car was raised. John walked around to look under the wheel. "You better watch," he said. "You worked your guardian angel pretty hard last night."

"Yeah, and that ain't half of it brother!" I started my confession.

I wouldn't have confided my misstep to anyone but John. He and I had been close friends for nearly three years. We first met when both of us skipped a lecture, a real feat considering the logistics. If you went to morning prayer and breakfast, then every one of your classmates saw you. The trick was to have something happen between breakfast and class, but there was only a 20–minute window of opportunity. You either had to look busy with something else, or appear to be experiencing spiritual angst—one so severe that you needed to visit your spiritual director. Most of the time, I would save my skips for the spring fishing season.

The day John and I met, we realized that, along with a shared aversion to attending classes, we both liked coffee and an occasional chew of snuff. It didn't take long before we became brothers, disciples, beer–drinking buddies, car mechanics, retreat companions and friends. Now my friend was listening to my confusing story of two masters. John listened quietly as I continued to fill in the details.

As painful as the retelling of the episode was, I needed to confide in someone—and who better than John? I trusted him. He and I often had long talks about God and Jesus and all the other spiritual issues that nourished our souls. This time we were talking in the garage. Other times it was in a local bar. John listened for some time, without saying too much; then, "Wow, a brake falling off and you didn't sleep with her—your guardian angel must be exhausted!"

I walked from the garage feeling thankful for my friend. I didn't know then that we would share a friendship for years to come. It would be John, who would vest me in the liturgical garb when I was ordained a Deacon. It would be John, who would stand beside me when I celebrated my first Mass.

In addition, it would also be John, who would stand beside my wife and me when he baptized our son.

CHAPTER X

The morning was gone but I cleaned myself up and managed to attend my afternoon class. When it was over, the vice rector, Father Benjamin was waiting for me in the hallway by the seminary offices. "Michael, do you have a minute?"

"Rip's in trouble," jeered two of my classmates in unison.

I thought Mom had died, and my heart started to race. Ben must have noticed my worried look. "It's nothing too serious; I just need to talk with you."

"I'll catch you guys later," I said and followed Ben into his office.

The silhouette of Ben's brown robe harkened my soul back to a different age. Some friars who wore them looked out of place. For Ben, it looked natural.

I had a great relationship with Ben. He was the only other friar who knew me as well as John. By my third year, he was appointed vice rector of the seminary and our friendship wasn't able to continue due to his new authority. Still, we chatted and shared a beer every now and then.

"Have a seat, Michael," he said, and closed the door behind me. He motioned to a worn, upholstered chair. The office was larger than most, with floor–to–ceiling books covering two walls. I noticed the complete works of psychotherapist Sigmund Freud alongside those of Catholic theologians Karl Rahner and Edward Schillebeeckx. A few worn theology books and journals were strewn about on the floor.

Sitting down I asked, "What's up?"

I tried to anticipate what I would hear next. I prayed he wouldn't ask about my missing the morning classes and I began to wonder if maybe he had called me in to reprimand me. A few weeks earlier, I attended an in–house symposium, visited by some out–of–town hierarchy. I pushed the limits by refusing to wear clerics and later heard it really bothered the Academic Dean.

"Michael, have you had anything unusual happen to you recently?"

I felt immediate relief. I wasn't in trouble. I breathed out and relaxed even more, as I sank back into the chair. "No—why?"

"Well, there has been a recent campaign to defame me. It came from within our community. Unfortunately, your name was involved."

I was floored. I was now a character in the middle of a monastic drama.

Ben continued, "I am sure that, among other things, this happened because this person did not want me to be in any position of authority. Not only did he want to defame me, but he also wanted to hurt other friars and, apparently you."

"Whoa, that's sick!"

"I'm sorry, Michael, that this involves you. Someone is investigating the letters and other happenings that don't involve you, but may be connected. Since this was a widespread campaign, I told your diocese."

The telephone in the outer office rang and jolted a memory of another phone call. Now it became perfectly clear. "You know, this past summer…" I said, and then paused. "This past summer, when I was at my deacon parish assignment, someone called and threatened to kill me if I didn't end my friendship with John."

"Tell me about it."

"Well, it was a summer evening and I was on the back deck with the other two priests. We were eating dinner when the telephone rang. One of them answered it and told me the call was for me. When I answered, a voice said, 'Stay away from John.' I asked, 'Who is this?' and the voice repeated, 'Stay away from John, or I will kill you.' "

Ben nodded slowly acknowledging the connection.

"I thought it was a joke." I glanced at Ben, feeling a little unnerved. "I guess it was real, huh?"

"I'm not sure, but we need to treat the threat as real. Michael, please lock your door."

I went back to my room and stared out the window at the mountain ridge just across the barren cornfields. In the distance was a bright orange sign for an adult bookstore flashing, LIVE NUDES. Apparently, the porn shop wasn't the only place where the demon took up residence.

I'm trying to keep it together, I mumbled to myself, hoping God was within earshot.

Mom was dying. I ran away to a hotel with a married woman last night. Today, I find out that some twisted friar really did threaten my life because of my friendship with John and Ben.

I hate my life! As soon as I thought it, I felt like I had cut my own heart. I knew it was wrong, but I wanted God to hear my tantrum.

I went to my medicine closet and grabbed two tablets for the migraine I was sure I would begin to feel any moment. I hoped they would provide relief from all my pain, but I knew no amount of pills would make that happen. I wished I were anywhere but here.

My mental blame game continued: *What a life! Thank you, Jesus!*.

I felt violated and vulnerable, angry and somewhat paranoid, all at once. This was sick! Why was I letting this bother me? Did this mean that the threat on my life was real? What if this crazed person did actually try to kill me? If Ben told the diocese, why didn't they call me and at least ask if I was okay?

I flopped down on my bed and fell asleep, pummeled by my fears, worries, hatreds and sins. I didn't know how long I had slept, when I heard footsteps outside my door. There was no reason for anyone to be at my end of the hall. I was in the last room. Jumping to my feet, I gagged on the extra saliva from my snuff. My pulse raced but my body wouldn't move. I froze, realizing I had forgotten to lock my door. Ben told me to lock my door—it was the last thing he told me to do—and yet, I forgot to do it.

Everyone was at the basilica for evening prayer and Mass; afterward, they would go to dinner. I guessed that I had been sleeping about an hour and a half. If that was true, everyone was having dinner in the refectory three buildings away, and I was alone in St. Anthony Hall. It was the perfect time to get rid of me.

They must have learned that Ben had told me everything. Now no one would be around to witness my murder. I thought of the movie *The Name of the Rose*, a mystery involving Franciscan friars and murder, and pictured some crazed friar going around killing people.

I heard a click. I watched the doorknob slowly turn. I grabbed my desk chair and held it high, ready to strike.

There was a knock. Someone slowly opened the door. "Rip?"

"Aahh." I swung the chair down to the floor.

Dan jumped back. "What's wrong with you?"

"Oh, crap. I thought you were..." I couldn't finish the thought.

"Is everything okay?" He shut the door behind him. "What's going on?"

I heard the other guys making their way down the hall and into their rooms. I had slept through Mass and missed dinner. One of the said, "Smitts and I haven't seen you since Ben called you in. Is your Mom okay?"

"Yeah." I couldn't say much more. I was still trying to calm down.

"You sure you're alright?"

"Yeah. What time is it?" I tried to change the subject.

"Almost seven. We thought something happened because Ben wasn't at dinner either. We thought maybe your had Mom died. Why did you almost hit me with a chair?"

I knew that Dan wouldn't stop asking questions. He honestly cared about people and did whatever he could to help. He would make a good priest. I wanted to tell him what was going on, but then decided it wouldn't help my situation.

"Hey, do you want to go get something to eat?"

"Mike, I just finished eating."

"Right. I knew that."

"You sure everything is okay?"

"Come on." I grabbed my jacket, keys, and snuff. "Let's go get something to eat."

"Rip. I already…" he said, and then stopped. "Okay, give me a second to get my coat."

Dan was a good friend. He arrived at St. Francis after his seminary in Kansas closed. He finished his last three years of formation here. It wasn't until a few months after his arrival, and after Smitts and I bought him a "welcome gift" for his fish tank that we became friends. I was surprised that he still wanted to be my friend after that gift. I had given him a plastic bag full of water and one colorful fish. "Maybe it's a tetra, I'm not sure." I had told him.

I didn't want to tell him what it really was. Later he discovered, after witnessing the new fish chew the fins off of the old fish, that, instead of a tetra, it was actually a piranha.

Dan was kind enough to watch me eat dinner and talk for several hours that night. On our return, he went to his room and I went to the chapel and sat on the floor, propping my back against the wall just to the side of the tabernacle. My eyes slowly adjusted to the dark and I could make out the outline of St. Clare in the stained–glass window. I watched as the flame of the red sanctuary candle flickered and broke the darkness in the room. Jesus was with me. I rested my head and soon fell asleep.

Later, I slowly opened my eyes and looked at the blurred image on the stained glass window. St. Clare was staring down at me. How pathetic I must have looked. My head was throbbing and my back was killing me from sleeping on the floor. I got up, genuflected and left the chapel.

It was morning. The community was waking, getting ready for another day of formation, prayer, and communal living. On the other hand, I had some insane friar threatening my life and possibly stalking me; and, a beloved mother nearing death. Maybe God had forgotten me.

I walked past Ephraim Freed's room. Eph always seemed to have it together, probably because he was older and wiser, having experienced more of life than I had. "Morning, Eph," I said strolling past his partly opened door. The smell of coffee emanated from his room.

"And how is Michael this lovely morning?"

I had met Eph two years earlier, when the vocation director from my diocese asked me to host a visitor, who was considering the seminary. All I knew was that he was a retired high school teacher. Eph had spent the day observing classes and praying with us. Later in the afternoon just before evening Mass, I remembered walking to his room and asking him directly: "So, did you decide? You gonna' become a priest or what?"

He had laughed at my humor, and entered the seminary the following semester. Eph, Ben, John, Danny and Smitts were my support group in those dark days. I was thankful for all of them.

I never found out who was behind the rumors and threats. Nothing more ever developed. Two weeks later, my father called with more grim news of my mother. Everything else now somehow seemed trivial.

I made the trip home, and my way into her hospital room. I gave my Dad, brother and sister a hug then pulled the chair alongside Mom's bed. She didn't notice me. She was gazing at the ceiling and gently striking her chest with her right hand. She did it three times saying, "mea culpa, mea culpa, maxima mea culpa." Mom was attending Mass—somewhere. I wondered if it was a memory of her going as a child with her family or maybe with us. Or, was she attending Mass in that thin place between Heaven and Earth—that place that she had seemed to exist in for the past couple of days?

I reached out, caressed her hair and rested my hand on her forehead, feeling the heat from her fever. She opened her eyes and smiled. She knew me, but right away I became afraid. This was our last moment to look into each other's eyes on this side.

I started to cry. "I love you Mom."

I barely got the words out. I rested my head on her chest as she laid her hand on my head, and slowly caressed my hair. I could hear her slowing heartbeat, and I held onto her. We both cried. "Michael…I love you, Michael."

That night, my mother died.

Twenty–three days later, I was ordained a deacon. Following the ceremony Dad gave me a gift from him and Mom—a gold wedding band that signified my marriage to Jesus Christ.

CHAPTER XI

I walked down the steps leading from the altar to the center of the church and stood before the congregation. Adjusting my deacon's stole, I smiled at the bride and groom kneeling on the prie–dieu just in front of the altar. They were my first couple. I had helped them through the entire process: the marriage prep meetings, the paperwork and interviews, the rehearsal, and now this, the day of their celebration of the Sacrament of Holy Matrimony.

"Did you ever notice how married couples look more and more like each other as time goes on?" There was a faint chuckle. "No, seriously, I mean it." I paused. "Come to think of it, I guess the same thing could be said about dogs and their owners." They laughed a little more.

"True love changes you, it transforms you and sometimes true love makes the lover and the beloved look like each other. The love story we celebrate today at this marriage is really a sign of the love story that God has with each one of our souls."

I continued, trying my best to preach what I truly believed. "You are to become God's lover. You are to become His cherished, sought–after spouse. And, just like a marriage, you will, as time goes on, take on the characteristics of your lover."

The words fell on my own deaf ears. My homily was wishful thinking. Never did I suspect during training that when I finally began preaching as a deacon I would also be experiencing doubts and questioning the very existence of God. It wasn't supposed to be this way. My faith was supposed to carry me, give me hope and sustainment. Now, I questioned everything I once believed.

During the final months of seminary, I drove every weekend from St. Francis to my weekend parish assignment at Our Lady of Joy, where I would attempt to 'plug' myself into the life of a local parish as a deacon. After the last Mass on Sunday, I would drive back to the seminary. It was as if I had no home. The arrangement resembled a judicial custody agreement.

At the same time, there was worry about what the future held for me as a diocesan priest. I had no idea where I would be stationed or with whom I would be living or what living environment I would encounter. It felt as if the custody agreement would soon morph into a placement in foster care, one in which I had no control. As a result, the good feelings of eagerness and joy once felt about being ordained a priest were replaced by worry and apprehension.

Part of me wanted to make the switch and enter the religious community at St. Francis. I felt I had a greater connection to them and their way of life than with my home diocese. I always thought I would make a good Franciscan.

As the last months of seminary ended, I tried to regain the feelings of that young boy barely able to see himself in the mirror, the child who had heard the call of the priesthood. For so many years, I had longed to be one with Jesus Christ—and still did. However, the inspiration was now only a memory. On the eve of ordination to the Holy Priesthood of Jesus Christ, I felt only one thing—a desire to be united to my God.

I yearned for one moment of that blessed assurance that He wanted me.

There was no way to let go now, though. I was convinced the only path to experience a union with Christ was through offering Holy Eucharist as His priest. I had to see it through and realize my doubts were nothing more than a spiritual dry spell. I would be ordained in the middle of a "Dark Night" of my soul.

The day of ordination finally came, ushered in with a knock at my door. "Michael?" I had not slept all night. "Michael?" The voice from the hallway sounded muffled.

"Yeah, just a minute," I hollered, making my way to the door to learn that my ordination classmate had locked himself out of his room. He asked me to climb out of my window, walk across the flat roof, enter through his window and unlock his door. That was how my ordination day began.

It was tradition that the ordinands, those about to be ordained, stayed overnight at a nearby convent of Franciscan sisters. I spent the night before my ordination in their chapel praying desperately for some affirmation from God. I did not sleep, I prayed. Hours later, I awoke lying prostrate on the cold marble sanctuary floor at Holy Name Cathedral, hearing the choir intone the Litany of Saints. Afterward, my friend Father Ben vested me in my priestly garb.

In contrast to the struggle going on inside of me, the ceremony itself was rather placid. There were no visions, no voices, and no affirmations—except for me reaffirming my commitment to celibacy.

I knelt in the sanctuary of the cathedral, and wished I felt the joy I had expected on this day, the culmination of years of study and the achievement of my lifelong goal. Instead I felt only resignation to what I believed was God's plan, and I remained convinced that I needed to follow the path I had decided on years ago. I linked all the mini–affirmations of God's call—my first Holy Communion, the crowning thorns in college, and the voice of God on retreat—and found what I thought was all the proof I needed. I prayed that day for a union with God. I wanted nothing more than to be His spouse.

Two weeks later, my spouse and I moved into my first parish assignment—St. Peter's Catholic Church.

the Confusion

1993–1995

"I have sinned; I, the shepherd, have done wrong."
—from 2 Samuel.

CHAPTER XII

On my first official day as the new assistant priest at St. Peter's Catholic Church, Pastor Jerry Lensosky handed me a set of keys and immediately set off on his summer vacation. The house was empty except for me.

I unpacked a few boxes of books and clothes and then headed across the parking lot to the church. The church building was connected to the school and offices, forming a parish complex. Forty years earlier when the place was built, the plan was to one day convert the church to a gymnasium for the school. That day never came and the church remained as originally built. I found a spot in the closet and hung my alb, the white tunic I used for Mass, and then carried my chalice over to the safe.

When I was in seminary, church catalog and chalice companies would bring their wares to sell—setting up tables like vendors at a home show. I never accepted the practice and did not buy a chalice. I was the only priest from my ordination class who did not have a brand new one. I used an old one given to me by the pastor from my deacon assignment.

Dad bought a small patent for the Host and had it engraved with the date of my ordination and the words 'from Mom and Dad.' I found a spot on a shelf to store them and left the sacristy.

I made my way down the school hallway lined with shiny pale catholic–green tile and arrived in the parish office. I sat down at my huge empty desk smelling of Murphy Oil Soap and looked at the phone. I fought the urge to call my Dad. I did not know if I was missing him or if just thinking of him all alone at home made me miss my mom.

Later that afternoon I sat alone on the back deck wood banister of the rectory eating a sandwich, washed down with a bottle of cold beer. While the sun beat down, a chorus of insects sang in the brush and dry grasses in the nearby field, adding some noise to the moment.

In addition to Jerry, there was a priest in residence, Father Phillip, whose ministry was to serve as chaplain at a home for troubled girls. He also was gone at least for the day. There I sat on the railing on my first day as a parish priest. After so many years, I had now achieved everything that I had thought, felt and prayed I was called to become.

So why did I feel so empty?

That night, I fell asleep in my sitting room on a dilapidated brown cloth recliner pockmarked with cigarette burns. Hours later, I was startled awake by the sound of an air–raid siren. Everything vibrated. The siren wailed and moved higher in pitch, held at a steady and ear–piercing level and then slowly descended.

At first, I thought it was somebody playing a joke on me. All day I was expecting a group of people to yell 'Surprise!' and make a fuss about my first day in the parish. I opened the window. No one was standing outside. No one yelled 'Surprise!' No one said 'Welcome!' The only sound interrupting the quiet of that hot summer night was the wailing siren.

I located the source of the sound—the firehouse's siren was attached to the telephone pole located next to the rectory. By my third year of living there, I would be able to sleep right through it—but not tonight. I put in a chew, sat back in the recliner and stared at the ceiling fan casting its shadows round and round. I closed my eyes and listened to the siren screaming for attention.

I had heard horror stories of new priests going to their first assignments. There was no real horror at St. Peter's. The only newsworthy event discussed was that the pastor before Jerry had left the priesthood. For the most part, things were rather quiet. I just did not know what to do for the first few months. Five years of seminary had not trained me on the specific day–to–day duties I should perform as a parish priest.

As a result, my days passed unscheduled. There was no structure to the day except for Morning Mass. It was not long before I stopped praying the morning and evening prayers I had always prayed throughout seminary. In fact, I had made a promise when I was a deacon that I would continue to pray the Liturgy of the Hours—specific prayers to be prayed each day at specific times. I had prayed in this way all through my seminary years, but now on my own, there always seemed to be some excuse not to do it.

Occasionally I would say night prayers in my room and fall asleep with a rosary, but soon that was replaced with staying up and watching the huge TV in the rectory's living room. I rationalized and explained away my laziness, saying that it was part of my adjustment and transition to parish life. I expected my prayer life to kick back into gear eventually. I seemed to be waiting for that to happen rather than working to make the shift take place. I rarely sat in church to pray. The only time I could go to church undisturbed was late at night. Yet it was not as convenient as going to the chapel in the seminary; in short, I grew lax in my pursuit of God.

One morning, after celebrating Mass and putting things away in the sacristy, I noticed the church was empty. I decided to sit in a pew for a while and pray. About 10 minutes later, feeling the presence of someone standing in the aisle next to my pew, I looked up and saw a woman looking at me.

"I'm sorry, Father, but I need to know something."

No wonder I have not attempted to pray in the church for months, I thought. Yet, something told me this was important; I could sense her emotion. "Please...have a seat."

Her eyes began to well up with tears. "Father, my brother was just diagnosed with AIDS."

"I'm sorry." Now I felt terrible for wanting to avoid this woman's intrusion into my prayer life; ten minutes of quiet would not have gotten me back on track anyway.

She paused to blow her nose. "I just need to know—when he dies, will he go to Hell?"

"Why would he go to Hell?"

"Well, because of his lifestyle."

I had no idea if he would go to Hell. I had been in diapers longer than I had been a priest. I did not feel equipped to answer the question. "Do you love him?"

"Yes, of course I do."

"Well, if you love him don't you think God loves him?"

"Yes."

"God doesn't want any of us to go to Hell. He does not send us there—we choose to go there. Help your brother choose God. Keep on loving him and help him surrender what he has left of his life to Jesus."

"Yes, alright," she said, hesitantly. "Thank you, Father."

I stood up to leave and had to add one more thing: "Don't damn your brother, love him."

I walked through the side door to the parking lot and out into the morning sun, and replayed my answer in my head: love, surrender, love the sinner, hate the sin, okay—good.

During that first year, the office of clergy for the diocese had the newly ordained meet several times to develop job descriptions. Not much time passed before I realized it was a foolish waste of energy. The fabulous job description I developed did little to improve my ministry or my focus. Instead, I became judgmental. The other priests were far less busy than I was, or so it seemed when I compared them to my 'written' self. I could not measure up to what the paper demanded and I quickly became overwhelmed. What the sentences detailed was clearly distant from reality; there was no hope for success. By the midpoint of my first year, I realized I had set myself up for job–description failure.

Within one year as a priest, I was already far removed from the image of my home parish priest, Monsignor Murphy, who had inspired me when he prayed the rosary before the Blessed Sacrament. Rather than describing my role as "on my knees praying," I wrote that I would "preside and lead congregational worship." Also absent was even one word about offering any sacrifice.

I was clearly moving in the wrong direction. I began concentrating more on process and program than on the fundamentals of being a priest. After five years of learning theology, I was now told I did not need as much as I had been given. Instead, what I needed most was organizational leadership.

Jesus, the CEO, replaced the Sacrificial Lamb.

I was consumed by psychosocial jargon and self–help books; soon, I began to accept the diocesan administrative language of self–actualization for its priests. More hope was placed in the science of man than in the love and compassion of God. Rather than seeking guidance from Holy Scripture, theology and prayer, it was easier to seek inspiration from a new reading list: *Seven Habits of Successful People*, *Re–founding the Church*, *The Dysfunctional Church*, *The Last Priests in America* and *Iron John*.

My new library no longer focused on devotion to Jesus Christ but rather on unfulfilled primal angst and agendas against the Roman Catholic Church. Disenchantment and disillusionment followed me everywhere, even to my first overnight clergy gathering. The celebration of Holy Eucharist and the communal praying of the Liturgy of the Hours were sandwiched between workshops on paradigm shifts. The breakout sessions amounted to little more than group therapy, dominated by the complaining of a few angry and quite vocal priests. I found the discussions corrosive to what I considered the very soul of priesthood.

That evening, I returned from the clergy gathering and opened the door leading from the garage to the basement. The strong smell of lacquer hit me, and I knew immediately it was Father Phil's doing. I felt my anger rising.

Everyone believed Phil had the gift of art. He lived in the basement, which he had transformed from its original old meeting room purpose into a post–Elizabethan era bedroom and sitting room. While I agreed it was very well done, I never appreciated his creativity. In my judging mind, he had created an alternate reality to avoid ministry.

As time went on, the people of the parish continued to love Father Phil, but I found myself increasingly convinced that Phillip had them fooled, having carved a niche for himself as the chaplain at the group home. He had the luxury of naming his own hours. From my perspective, his ministry—celebrating Mass twice a week and occasionally having office hours—was a walk in the park.

The smell of lacquer grew stronger as I reached the top of the stairs and stood in the kitchen. So did my anger. What was he doing spraying lacquer in the middle of winter in a closed house, I grumbled to myself as I walked down the hall to my room. So began the litany of complaints against Phil, who was now the scapegoat for my sins and for me in general.

I showered and made my way back to the kitchen, where Jerry and Phil were busy heating frozen dinners in the microwave. Phil always tried to avoid meeting anyone in the kitchen. Usually he would run upstairs, grab his food and then retreat to his basement room to eat. It was rare for the three of us to mingle in the kitchen but this time there was no escaping the inevitable.

I fired first: "Nice smell, Phil. I enjoy the suffocating stench of lacquer in the middle of winter."

His eyes changed to a squinty glare. Jerry's grew large and he moved back against the doorway that led into the dining room. "Well, your motorcycle exhaust gives me a headache," Phil retorted.

It was my open. "You want exhaust? I'll drive the bleeping bike into your girly room right now!"

"You think you're tough, you're nothing but a kid."

I clenched my fist. I wanted to punch him.

"Now guys..." Jerry began a quiet attempt at calming us, but was cut off.

"You stay out of this!" Phil shouted.

"I'm just a kid?" With that, I grabbed him by his shirt and pushed him back against the counter. "I'm just a kid?" I started pushing my finger into his chest. "What the hell, Phil, every time I turn around I hear about 'poor' Father Phillip. You have them all convinced you're overworked or dying, or both!"

"Do you want to hit me?" He lifted his chin, playing the role of the victim to the fullest. "Go ahead, if you want to. If it makes you feel better, go ahead."

I let go of Phil's shirt and wiped the saliva from the corners of my mouth. Jerry said nothing as he turned and walked through the dining room and out of the front door. I walked into the sitting room and angrily plopped down on the brown recliner. The phone rang. I gathered myself as best I could. "Hello, St. Peter's, this is Father Michael."

"Hello, Father. Sorry to disturb you, but can you tell me what time confessions are tomorrow?"

CHAPTER XIII

Within my first year of priesthood, three things were accomplished: becoming disillusioned; starting a sexless, but nevertheless, adulterous relationship; and, entering psychotherapy—in that order.

Ashley Jenson was Director of Religious Education at a nearby parish. Both our parishes shared some of the responsibilities for faith formation and catechesis, the religious instruction usually done before Baptism or Confirmation. It was standard practice for the two of us to have weekly interaction. What started innocently ended sinfully.

It was not long before Ashley started sharing with me that she was unhappy in her marriage. She made the mistake of sharing too much about her marital difficulties and I made the mistake of listening.

Ashley and I became more comfortable sharing our lives and even our complaints with one another—she, her marriage; me, the priesthood. It was only a matter of time before our conversations included occasional jokes about sex. Then, one Saturday afternoon, everything changed.

We were at a diocesan workshop and during a break, she grabbed me in the hall and said, "I have to tell you something."

"Okay, Ash." I moved closer.

Ashley stood against the wall and whispered, "I was with him, you know, but..." she paused, looking up and down the hallway to see if anybody was in earshot. "But I kept my eyes closed and pretended it was you."

I was floored. Then I was drawn in by the attention, which I secretly enjoyed. It was so easy for me to rationalize what was quickly unfolding. Perhaps it was the extreme solitude I had been experiencing during my first year as a new priest that made me forget this kind of involvement was sinful. I felt myself being drawn toward the flirtation.

We didn't talk for a week after that. The next Saturday I heard confessions, then went back in the sacristy to get things ready for evening Mass. The door opened and Ashley walked in. She came over and stood next to me, closer than usual. "Hey, Ash," I said glancing her way.

"I thought I'd find you here," she said, adding a sigh.

"Yep." I placed unconsecrated hosts in the large ciborium. "You here for the RCIA meeting?"

"Yeah." She moved closer. "Michael?"

"Yes." I fumbled with setting the ribbons in the Sacramentary book for Mass.

"I...I don't know how long it's going to last with us."

"What?" I turned and looked at her. "What do you mean, last with us? You mean you and Henry?"

"Yeah."

"Well, what is it you want?"

She moved closer and pushed her body against me. "This." She dropped her papers and we embraced.

In an instant, I somehow gave myself permission to feel the attraction. It was just a hug, wasn't it? It lasted maybe a total of 30 seconds—but as quickly as I had granted myself permission, I started taking it away. What was I doing? We were in the sacristy and this wasn't some kind of cute affirming hug; it was sexual. What was wrong with me?

I backed away and excused myself from the room. Two hours later, I celebrated Mass.

That night I sat in my room at the rectory and again rationalized what had happened. My year wasn't actually shaping up to be the religious experience of priesthood I had envisioned. Maybe Ashley and I were using each other for emotional support. We stroked each other's egos and tried to help solve each other's problems.

I liked having a woman's presence in my life, which I justified as a way to get through a difficult time. Even the lust was justified because, I rationalized, I knew how to control it. We didn't hug again; thus, in my mind, there was no sin. I became my own judge and played the role of the frustrated celibate, while Ashley played the unhappily married woman. The Hollywood drama of the scene drew me in and kept me coming back.

We were using each other and yes, I did know it was wrong. I searched for every plausible excuse to justify my actions and feelings for Ashley: my unmet expectations and frustrations as a new priest and, of course, the biggest excuse of all, God not answering my prayers of uniting me in some mystical way to His Being. It was so easy to blame my life on God. It was even easier to lose my ability to make correct judgments.

Several weeks later, I temporarily lost my moral compass. Late one afternoon I drove my motorcycle over to Ashley's apartment while her husband was still at work. We sat outside on the concrete porch stoop talking about nothing and watching the occasional car go by.

We both used the excuse of being thirsty to go inside for a drink. I stepped into the house and Ashley followed behind me. I turned and watched her shut the door. She stared at me, then reached behind her back and locked the deadbolt.

I never had anyone want me this much. Ashley unbuttoned her blouse and slowly walked toward me. Within minutes, we had our shirts off and were on the floor of the living room, touching, caressing and teasing each other. I wanted her to want me, and I didn't stop to think about what it would do to her, her husband or their marriage. I didn't stop to think about what it would do to me—or my priesthood.

Outside a car pulled up and the engine quit—right in front of the house.

"Oh my God, he's home!" she said. Jumping up, she grabbed her blouse from the floor and ran upstairs to the second floor. She was gone, and I was left standing shirtless in the living room. My mouth went dry and I felt my heart beating.

"Crap," I mumbled. "Where's my shirt?"

I ran into the kitchen, pulled back the drapes on the sliding glass door and desperately fumbled for the handle. I unlatched it, but it wouldn't slide open.

I heard a key opening the lock on the front door. Ashley's husband walked into the kitchen and saw me frantically trying to get the door to slide. I looked over my shoulder and our eyes met. He turned and walked upstairs.

I heard the two of them whispering. There was no shouting or yelling; they were just whispering. The thought crossed my mind, just for a moment, of trying to talk myself out of this. We should not have done what we did, but it was just shirts, right? It was just shirts.

I decided to walk out the front door and leave. I turned the knob and for a split second stared at the unlocked deadbolt. I closed the door quietly behind me and walked over to my motorcycle as if nothing had happened. I hopped on my bike and headed back to the parish. At an intersection, a parishioner honked his horn and waved. I read his lips. "Hey, Father Mike!"

I waved back and realized—I wasn't wearing a shirt.

That night, I packed the leather saddlebags on the motorcycle and headed north. I didn't have to be back at the parish for two days. I had no idea where I was going until I ended up in a field along a rural section of U.S. Route 30, just outside of New Oxford. I lay on a saddle blanket and stared up at the stars. Nobody knew where I was and for a wonderful moment, I felt complete freedom.

Suddenly, the reality of all the darkness and sin of my life surrounded me. I knew better than to get involved with Ashley. I knew that being at her home was incredibly immoral and I would have to make amends to her and her husband. I just wasn't sure how or when. One thing I knew for sure, I would not be alone with her again.

Looking up at the stars and feeling the weight of all that had happened, I uttered a prayer, "Mom, I need help."

CHAPTER XIV

The first year of my priesthood finally ended. To celebrate the milestone, I met some of my classmates for a reunion at a small cabin in the middle of Pennsylvania. A lot had happened to me in that year. I wondered if anyone else was hiding secrets. I couldn't shake the feeling that I was a fraud as a priest.

The reunion lasted about three days. There were card games, cigars smoked and many stories about bishops, pastors and the people of God; all was told from the viewpoints of young priests, and all was washed down with a beer or two.

Mike Smitts, one of my close friends in school, seemed distant and on edge with everyone and everything. He had lived through some difficult times. His father died when he was in college, and his brother died while we were in seminary. When I lost my Mom, we seemed to connect even more as members of a special club; not many students our age already had a deceased parent.

Smitts and I lived right next to each other for a period of four years during seminary. In our first year of priesthood, we had never gotten together. I just became overwhelmed making all the transitions and adjustments and forgot to stay connected to friends and their support.

It was easy to become isolated as a young priest. From the outside looking in, parishioners saw priests attending many different church functions, always surrounded by people. However, no one saw what happened after the functions ended. The parishioners returned to their homes and families, while the priest returned to the rectory—alone. After leading Vigil prayers at the funeral home, the priest returned to the rectory—alone. After the celebrating a wedding, the priest returned to the rectory—alone. After Sunday Masses and weeknight meetings had come and gone, the priest returned to the rectory—alone. After all I did as a priest—I was alone.

Smitts decided to leave the reunion a day early. The rest of us watched the cloud of dust swirl up from his car, which made its way down the dirt road. Danny Crucis, started to pace back and forth in front of us. It was a choppy, nervous pacing. Then, out of nowhere, like he was carrying on a full conversation with us in his head, Dan blurted, "He asked me not to tell anyone...."

The rest of us just looked at each other. "What are you talking about, Dan?" I reached in my pocket, pulled out a can of Copenhagen and tapped on the lid.

"He's probably going to leave...Smitts, he's leaving," Dan said, and then kept talking as if we were interrogating him. "He's going to leave or take a leave, or something." Dan kept spewing information. "There's a girl."

Someone opened the cooler and started passing out beer. I snapped mine open and slurped the froth. "Lucky guy."

"He asked me not to say anything."

"Come on Dan!" I said. "He told you. Think about it. He wants us to know. He told you!"

Dan continued his discourse. "They've been together for a while, hanging out at the rectory."

"For how long?" I asked.

"Almost a year."

"You gotta be kidding me! One year? He's only been ordained for a year!"

I acted as if I had the right to act scandalized. I wondered if it was love. If so, I was jealous. The stone that I held ready to cast at Smitts was really a stone I wanted to throw at myself. My first year as a priest had been terrible and I had no one to blame but myself.

We stood around and talked about Mike leaving the priesthood. Everyone had a sidebar opinion, until the mother of all comments was spoken: "He probably shouldn't have even been ordained."

Priests have a way of casting out one of their own, as if the one who left suddenly became a cancer that had to be removed.

With the car's dust now long settled, we went back to our reunion. At that moment, I had no way of knowing that years later, Smitts and I would 'illegally' concelebrate Palm Sunday Mass with our wives and children.

CHAPTER XV

With friendships renewed and the holiday over, we set off in our separate directions, each moving on to contemplate the meaning of all that had been spoken in our days together.

I continued to pray and ask for guidance. A couple of months later, the answer to my prayers seemingly started to unfold. The full answer would not be revealed to me for many years, but I started to believe that perhaps the Virgin Mary, the Mother of God, had taken over on that fateful night in the field when I had asked my own mother for help.

It began when my friend Father Mark Haugnstott phoned to invite me to travel with him to Mexico City to visit the Shrine of Our Lady of Guadalupe. Apparently, he also needed something to jumpstart his priesthood and I had nothing to lose by going. Even though the "affair" with Ashley ended as quickly as it began, I was still living with the everyday awareness of that sin. We rarely spoke after that day in her home. I didn't know what else to do except stay away and enter psychotherapy. Not a day went by that I did not hate myself for what I had done. Mark's invitation was a desperately needed opportunity to get away from it all.

The story of the Shrine of Our Lady of Guadalupe dated back to 1531. A peasant named Juan Diego had a vision of the Virgin Mary who told him to build a church in the Mexican desert near Mexico City. The local bishop asked Diego for proof that Mary had appeared to him. The Virgin instructed Juan to gather some nearby roses blooming in the dead of winter into his cloak, or 'tilma,' which he laid on the ground before her. She then arranged them and sent him on his way to the bishop. When he opened his tilma in front of the bishop the roses cascaded onto the floor, leaving behind the image of Our Lady imprinted forever on his garment.

That colorful image, the miracle of God's painting of the Virgin Mary so many years before on a peasant's tilma woven of cactus fibers, has defied the natural order of nature and has not decayed. It is enshrined at the Basilica of Our Lady of Guadalupe for all to see. I traveled to the site with the desperate hope that the Virgin Mary would help me get back on track. I needed a spiritual imprint.

The night we arrived in Guadalupe a priest showed us to our rooms. I walked into the bathroom, poured water from the porcelain pitcher into a basin and splashed it over my face. I grabbed a hand towel and dried off, and then walked across the mosaic–tiled floor towards an open window, resting my arms on the window sill and looking outside. My eyes were drawn to a nearby hillside where I noticed four larger–than–life statues. The moon shone directly behind them.

The scene sent a chill through my body. I had seen it before in a dream just a few weeks earlier. At the time, it had seemed real as dreams often do. Now, I wondered again if it had been more than a dream.

I had been asleep in my rectory bedroom. When I opened my eyes, I saw a man standing by my bed, as if waiting for me to awaken. I opened my eyes. He had long, shiny black hair. He smiled at me, but did not speak. Feeling no fear, I moved from my bed to the middle of the room, which was transforming into a cave. He led me up a narrow, ancient–looking circular staircase made of stones. Once at the top, we walked onto a turret. The familiar sites at the rectory had been replaced with a hillside and silhouettes of four enormous statues, overlooking some sort of ancient civilization. A full moon shone brightly from behind the statues. At that moment, I realized the man was an angel. When I asked his name, he said it was the same as mine. Then the dream ended.

The next morning, I began celebrating Mass, and opened the Sacramentary Book to see the prayers of the day. I was shocked at what I saw: September 29, The Feast of St. Michael the Archangel.

Seeing the statues before me, I was spiritually startled. I knew deep inside that the dream was real. I stared at the hillside for a long time. Maybe God hasn't forgotten me, I thought.

The next morning, Mark and I made our way to the Basilica. The place was filled with pilgrims, mostly natives. A constant drone of prayer in a language I didn't understand filled the air; somehow, I felt it. The smells of incense and sewage permeated the space.

I knelt on the conveyor belt, which slowly moved under the miraculous image of the Blessed Virgin on the tilma hanging a mere 20 feet above me. There, before the image of Our Lady of Guadalupe, I renewed my desire for a union with Christ. I wished at that moment that I could imprint the Virgin Mary on my soul just as it had been imprinted on the peasant's tilma. In the midst of so many people, I felt completely anonymous and found it easy to pour out my heart.

the Unraveling

1995 – 1997

"My soul is deprived of peace, I have forgotten what happiness is, I tell myself my future is lost, all that I had hoped for from the Lord."
—from the Book of Lamentations.

CHAPTER XVI

The intercom in my office clicked. "Father Michael, you have a phone call on line one. It's the Chancery," my secretary Paula said, her voice sounding nervous.

Receiving a call from the administrative offices of the diocese often had that unnerving effect on people. "Well, this is it." It was my best attempt at sounding light and cheery.

The phone call was a vital, yet meaningless step in the convoluted process known as priest transfers. The time that elapsed from the phone call to the actual first 24 hours at the new parish was usually about three weeks. The process made reality television look anemic.

"Hello, this is Father Michael." I tried to swallow past the lump in my throat. I was put on hold.

I knew the call would be coming. My current pastor, Father Jerry was well connected when it came to finding out who was to be assigned where. It was almost as if he had an inside line to the Chancery. The rectory phone had been ringing off the hook for the past two days; just about every hour on the hour, one of Jerry's priest informants would check in with the latest news or gossip, depending on your perspective.

A few months before, I had met with Auxiliary Bishop William Graeylo, hoping I might actually have a say in where I would be assigned. I had asked him to consider moving me into another type of ministry, something other than parish work. I hadn't revealed my personal issues in adjusting to parish life, but had tried to convince him that I would do better in another setting, perhaps one that wasn't parish ministry. I was even willing to go back to school.

Despite what I thought were good reasons, the bishop had bluntly said no, explaining he needed parish priests. I left the meeting believing that he didn't care about my needs and wondering if it would make more sense for me to call it quits and join the Franciscans.

I sat and nervously awaited a human voice on the phone and thought about what I had learned in my three short years as an assistant priest. All the lessons pointed in one direction. I did not want to be a parish priest; better yet, I simply could not be a parish priest. Considering my personal failures, I decided that the best solution was to leave parish ministry, but not the priesthood. I had lost my direction and no longer advanced on the holy quest that I had been pursuing for years—a union with Jesus Christ.

After the sins of my first year, I couldn't help but wonder if God had abandoned me, finding me unworthy of a mystical marriage and union with Christ. I longed for another ministry and way of living the priesthood that would support my holy pursuit of His love. While I was able to function in the parish and successfully perform the duties required—preaching, initiating new programs, leading discussions and general pastoral caring—there was still an empty part of me that was left wanting.

A woman's voice on the line startled me out of my reflection. "Father, please hold for the bishop."

I wondered if the bishop was really so busy that he couldn't dial the phone for himself. There I sat on hold thumping my fingers on the desk. Perhaps there was a glitch. It was late afternoon and as a lowly assistant priest, I was probably one of his final calls of the day; pastors, administrators and educators were usually the first to be notified. Maybe I even had the honor of being the final call of the year. Perhaps I was the last one bagged and the bishop was closing out the transfer season with me.

I sat staring out the window, waiting for a voice to speak to me. I started a mental replay of my meeting with the bishop. I had suggested I return to school to study spirituality and psychology, to work as an assisting clergy helping other priests who felt disconnected or disillusioned. However, the decision must have been no, or I would have been advised before now to start looking at graduate schools. The process of transfers had begun months ago at the Chancery. Like a game of cascading dominoes, each priest was lined up waiting for the push and the administration would watch to assure that each one fell as planned. It was called being obedient.

I was still on hold.

I looked at the clock on my desk. It had been a gift from the first couple I had married; they divorced within the first year and thankfully, I hadn't had anything to do with the demise of their marriage. The clock had the date of the wedding and "Fr. Mike" engraved on the brass plate. The hands no longer moved, because I had never replaced the battery.

I waited for the bishop's voice. In a matter of minutes, he would ask about my well–being, say how difficult the past few days have been for him—and then tell me where I was going. He would conclude by sharing that he would pray for me. After the call, I would have two weeks to get my affairs in order, uproot myself, move my belongings, pay for any and all expenses incurred out of my $1,000 monthly salary, show up, smile, act happy and Christ–like and be the greatest priest the parish had ever seen.

I was startled by a click on the phone. "Hello, Mike? How are you?"

"Fine, Bishop."

"You know, Mike," he said, hesitating as if he wasn't sure which assistant he had on the line, as if he were reading a piece of paper that had 'n' where each priest's name was to be inserted, "The last few days have been very difficult for me...."

CHAPTER XVII

"Steve, I can't go there," I yelled into the phone. "What the heck is he thinking? You know I need something more right now. I can't go to Holy Cross with Ron. This sucks!"

Father Steve Drundner was my mentor four years preceding my summer seminar and deacon assignments. Now he was my only hope. The bishop had spoken and I was headed to Holy Cross.

I wanted someone to listen to my reasons for not wanting to be transferred to Holy Cross. First, the rectory was also home to the parish offices; thus, the priests had no personal space. Second, all lunches and morning coffees were taken with the secretaries and housekeeper. Third, there were no regular staff meetings. In short, I would be living and eating with the staff on a daily basis and working with no structure for communication.

I had a bad feeling about the whole thing.

There was not one good reason why I should put myself in that situation. I had been told by the diocese for the past 11 years I had a right to expect a normal living situation and administrative leadership. Adding to my negatives, the pastor, Father Ron had a reputation in priest circles of being a drinker. I chose to believe it and also to use his alleged drinking as the primary argument against my assignment to Holy Cross. I was banking on it.

"Steve, what should I do?"

Steve knew all too well what I was saying. During my time with him, he was always concerned about the need for the diocese to hold clergy more accountable for their personal, pastoral and administrative actions. He was silent for a moment, then spoke, "It's about time we as a diocese address these issues. The bishop needs to hear from you that you need something different."

I had hope. Maybe my gut feeling had actually been correct. Maybe the informal circles of rumors had a grain of truth, and guys like Steve were willing to help reform problems in the diocese. Maybe he would practice what he preached.

Within one week, Steve, Pastor Ron and I were sitting in the auxiliary bishop's office. The bishop began, "So, Mike, I understand you have some concerns about going to Holy Cross."

He addressed me, so I was the one who had to initiate the true meaning of the meeting. I cleared my throat and leaned forward ready to deliver my well–rehearsed words: Bishop, first, we need to consider different opportunities and possibilities of ministry for me. Second, we need to take the blinders off and be honest about dysfunctional and unhealthy clergy living situations, which may involve alcohol and other addictions. We need to name these things. We need a paradigm shift. In fact, your office had me sit through a workshop on clergy health and paradigm shifts, remember?

I believed these words—but I didn't speak them. Instead, thoughts raced through my mind as I settled on other words: "Bishop, I have concerns, not just for me but for other priests."

The bishop seemed to look right past me.

"Steve?" I turned to my left to look at him. I needed his help to corroborate what he had said to me earlier; Steve now wouldn't even make eye contact with me. He just looked forward, frozen in place, like a schoolboy in the principal's office. I kept talking in his direction: "Steve, you said when I called you, 'It's about time we as a diocese deal with these issues.'"

Steve looked forward past the bishop and out the window. He coughed, cleared his throat and said nothing—not one word.

Anger filled me. Why wasn't Steve supporting me? Six months before, I had attended some sort of group counseling session concerning alcohol with him as his guest. In truth, when he shared the issue with me, I completely understood. I made mistakes, too. I turned to women. Now I wondered if this was the same person I had helped.

Steve didn't look at me when he finally did speak: "Bishop, I said no such thing."

I was stunned. I had entered the meeting expecting to change the way things were done and do something positive for the priesthood, the Church and me. It was not going to happen today.

The bishop began to fill the uncomfortable moment with talk about how difficult it is for him to make transfers, and about some assistant priest in the 1950s who wanted his own garage. I heard the bishop equate my concerns with "please give me a garage," and I started to shut down. I lost track of the conversation, felt sorry for Ron and was angry with Steve. I felt betrayed.

That evening I received a call from my spiritual director, Father Stanley. He was keeping tabs on the matter, yet I fully expected him to limit his involvement because the friendships were just too close. "Why don't I set up a meeting with you and Vince? He said, "If anything, at least you can let him know what wasn't said at the meeting with the bishop."

"That's fine if you think it's a good idea."

I hung up the phone. As director of personnel for the diocese, Vince knew that I had been dealing with my own issues since my first year. I had needed some money for therapy, so his office had paid for several visits. He didn't know the particulars, but I assumed he thought I was putting forth effort and trying to be a good priest.

So far in the game of transfer, calculating the stats for someone going to bat for me, I was zero for one. All I wanted was for one of my mentors to take a stand and convince the administration that I did not fit the parish priest psyche. It didn't seem like so much to ask.

A few days passed and our meeting was held at a local restaurant. I shared the entire story, from supporting Steve to my concerns about living with Ron. Vince and Stan wore their best poker faces. I became painfully aware that they had no idea about Steve. My motive was not to get Steve in trouble. It was simple and selfish—I didn't want to be in a parish.

Vince presented his solution: "Go and keep a record of anything you think we might need to know."

That was it. There was no mention of my assignment being changed and no concern from the diocese, my mentor or my spiritual director. Though I had hoped someone would take a stand and say, "Michael shouldn't go there," I realized I had been naive from the start; no one was going to face job peril for a brother priest—especially men in authority—who had worked hard to achieve their positions. The truth was that I simply wasn't worth the risk.

Thanks to the process, my eyes were opened to the realities of denial that existed in the Church. The priests I had trusted to go to bat for me were not going to risk their careers. The priests who advocate psycho–spiritual health of the clergy were simply not going to help me. I was not sure what the real intention of the meeting was that day. I began to wonder what else was being ignored.

Three weeks later, I sat in the rectory of Holy Cross alone at a wobbly wooden kitchen table eating a chicken salad sandwich on stale bread, obedient to my bishop's request. I parted the window's 1970 vinyl–backed curtains, covered with a garish geometric black, brown and yellow design to study my surroundings. A couple of acres of pavement weaved around the school, church and rectory buildings.

Ron was my new pastor, but he wasn't around. Just as before, I spent the first day at my new assignment alone.

Holy Cross was one of the largest parishes in the diocese, composed largely of suburban developments, strip malls and urban sprawl from D.C. In priest jargon, the parish was a sacrament factory. Simply put, my job was to "hatch 'em, match 'em and dispatch 'em" (also known as baptize, marry and bury). All that was expected of the priest was to just show up and not ask questions.

Along with the five Sunday Masses at Holy Cross there was also a Mass at a mission church, St. Agatha, situated nearby among old strip mines and boarded–up homes just on the border of Virginia. The priest scheduled to celebrate the Mass was required to drive a well–worn van over to the old folks high rise, help the old ladies into the van, drive past the main church to the mission church (where no more than 10–15 people attended) and then provide return taxi service when Mass ended. Every week I marveled that no one noticed the lack of efficiency in the plan.

After finishing my sandwich, I carried my chalice, alb and vestments over to the church. I slowly moved about in the sacristy, making myself familiar with all the necessities of being a priest on any given Sunday or weekday—like how to turn on the microphones, where the light switches were and, most importantly, where the key to the tabernacle was hidden.

I left the sacristy and meandered around the altar and podium and took a seat in the priest's chair staring out at the empty pews; there had to be at least two hundred of them. I tried to imagine how I would go about celebrating Mass. I liked to preach standing in front of the altar, but there wasn't enough room here for that approach. I stood up, genuflected and meandered halfway back to a pew, took a seat and sighed.

I stared at the tabernacle and did a little spiritual self–check. Surprisingly, I was no longer angry or sad. Leaving St. Peter's wasn't really that hard; in reality it had been freeing. Now, alone in the church, it was just me and Jesus once again, with His peace washing over me. I didn't expect it. Considering how the past few weeks had played out, the fact that I was even at Holy Cross was a miracle, let alone the Holy Presence that now enveloped me.

I closed my eyes and immersed myself in my surroundings. This was my new home. I leaned forward and placed my forehead on the back edge of the pew in front of me, saying, "Oh God, just be with me. Help me to believe that you sent me here."

I opened my eyes and looked at the crucifix, feeling strangely at peace.

God can help me work through all of this, I thought, He can and He will.

That night I hung a picture of Our Lady of Guadalupe in my bedroom.

Hail Mary, full of Grace…pray for me…

CHAPTER XVIII

During my time at Holy Cross, every day began and ended the same way. In the morning, the secretary would pull her car into the garage beneath my bedroom. I would awaken to the sound of the garage door, and see the sunlight breaking through the cheap plastic louvered blinds. I would lay motionless, staring at the ceiling, take a deep sigh and whisper in prayer, "Bow down and touch me Lord."

I felt as if I had to prepare for battle each day, so it was fitting that I spoke a prayer like the one from **Gettysburg**, one of my favorite movies. In a scene before the battle, Gen. Robert E. Lee, played by Martin Sheen, walks by his tent in the early morning; a narrator speaks a prayer: "Bow down Thy hands, Lord, and touch the earth, make my arms strong and ready for battle."

My daily battle was certainly less historic and bloody than General Lee's, but nevertheless, it required a morning prayer.

At night, in the living room above my bedroom, the pastor would camp out with his rum and cokes and watch the 750-inch JumboTron television. Then, around 11:30, he would shut it off and walk down the steps, which shared the wall with my bedroom. Only after I heard the outside basement door slam, would I be able to fall asleep.

I didn't fully know it at the time, but I had stepped into what would become the slow unraveling of my priesthood. I lived alone in a rectory complex originally the home for five priests but now only a shell of its former self that could best be described as a brick shack. I often wondered what my experience would have been had I lived back in the day when there was a community of men, living and working together for the Kingdom of God.

I judged and condemned the powers that had ignored my pleas and locked me away in this dead–end prison. I was spiritually rotting, slowly and silently, unnoticed by the world.

As I had been asked to do, I kept a written record of all the things that would prove my case. I recorded the times Ron would be drinking at night and then drive to his apartment. I recorded the weeks that would go by with no communications or meetings. The more details I entered into the record, the more depressed I became. I got a puppy, a black lab I named Jeb, hoping that some preoccupation with having to care for a dog would keep me from naval gazing.

Within the first year at Holy Cross, I applied for a transfer to a small parish that became available. It was tucked away in the mountains and away from the suburbs and city. It was at the other end of the diocese. I wanted a place to pursue God and follow my path to a mystical union, a quest I had temporarily suppressed.

Weeks went by and I didn't hear any word from the Chancery. Within the walls of my isolation, I concluded that I was nothing to them but an expendable priest, one they would never take seriously. I questioned authority and God. Had I fabricated my call to the priesthood just to make myself feel something?

Had I really been called to become a priest?

CHAPTER XIX

There were many dark days at Holy Cross, but the worst began very early one morning near my one–year anniversary. It was during a meeting at the Chancery to share my "report" with the personnel director.

I sat facing him. I couldn't help but notice how nice his office was. A twinge of jealousy overtook me. I wondered if he lived in a rectory that suffered from maintenance neglect and if his shower floor had ever fallen through as mine had a few days earlier. I refocused, took a deep breath, and looked him in the eyes. "Okay, you asked me to keep a record and let you know how things have been going."

The director just stared at me. "Well, here it is." I offered him the file folder. He would not take it, or even touch it. He uncrossed his legs, planted both feet solidly on the floor, and folded his arms. His defenses were up.

Finally, the director responded. "Why don't you just tell me what is in there?"

I did a cursory rundown of my parish experiences during the past year, highlighting Ron's drinking; but it didn't matter. His initial reaction had said it all. He listened and then turned his palms upward stating, "There is nothing we can do until he wants to help himself."

"Wha…What?"

"Mike, we can't force a guy to get help. I can't just move you because of what you think is wrong. If that were the case, we'd be moving guys nonstop."

Deep down, I had known it would go this way. I had heard the stories before and had even heard that line before. Still, it was wrong. The system should include strategies to help priests in need, to show care and concern before someone was killed while driving drunk. At that moment, on that day, I started losing respect for the institution I pledged to serve. I walked away with the understanding that neither Ron nor I really mattered we were both expendable.

With what little self–respect remained, I left the Chancery and took my time driving to Holy Cross. On the way, I took a familiar detour into the arms of a woman. I needed someone to comfort me and listen to my complaints. That someone was Lisa, a friend who knew me long before I was ordained. She welcomed me and listened to me complain. Her caring responses fed my ego. I had arrived defeated and now was becoming defiant.

What happened next was so subtle and rational it appeared to be excusable. We started chatting in the living room and eventually I stretched out on the floor, exhausted from my morning experience. "You need a back rub, you're all stressed," Lisa said, as she sat down beside me and started massaging my back. It was not just a back rub and I knew it.

I had always dismissed the occasional flirtatious gestures and words that were exchanged with Lisa between us through the years as good-natured fun, and maybe even a showing of support. However, once again, I was overextending and perforating the moral and ethical boundaries. The relationship was headed down the wrong path, one I didn't want to travel again.

Suddenly, a switch went off and we just stopped, slowly separating and careful not to look into each other's eyes. The day had started badly and was sinking to new lows.

There are countless stories of saints and holy men who endured a lifelong struggle with their passions. They were known to practice self-mortification and flagellation to curb their physical desires. While I had always considered such acts as pure insanity, I was beginning to understand why they would go to such extremes; my unbridled appetites were leading me away from God. On that dark day, I finally faced what I had become—a failed priest. I knew I had done this to myself.

That night in my bedroom, I knelt before the picture of Our Lady of Guadalupe, and yearned for a thorn bush in which to throw myself for punishment and for rebirth. I felt I was no longer worthy to live as a priest.

I stared at the image of Our Lady of Guadalupe hanging on my wall. "I need you," I whispered softly, "I need a miracle. Mary, help me..."

CHAPTER XX

The darkness of night gave way to a bright morning sun. The air was cool and crisp, filled with the aromas of a spring morning. My personal crisis would have to wait for a few days. It was the morning of Holy Thursday.

I finished putting on my priestly garments and stood outside under the covered corridor that connected the cathedral with its rectory. Priests from all over the diocese were gathering to celebrate the annual Chrism Mass, meant to signify the unity of the priests with their bishop.

The bishop would bless three silver urns of oil the Oil of Catechumen, the Oil of the Sick, and the Sacred Chrism used in the administration of sacraments throughout the diocese for the year. The priests of the diocese would also be renewing their promises made at ordination. In the religious order of things, this ceremony was a big deal.

Moving from the shade of the corridor to the parking lot and into the sunlight, I stared at an orange traffic cone that reserved the parking spot for the auxiliary bishop, who had yet to arrive.

For a second, my passive–aggressive self thought about moving it just to spoil his morning. He was an easy target to blame for my problems.

I felt a hand on my shoulder and turned to greet my friend Eph. "Hey Rip," he said, smiling back at me. I had not seen Ephraim Freed in at least a year, most likely since Chrism Mass last year.

"How's it going up there in…where are you?"

"Hanover, Rip, and it's going fine—you?"

"It's alright," I said, wishing I could tell the truth.

Eph's face suddenly lit up. "Hey, what are you doing on Monday?"

Before I could answer, a surreal silence descended on the scene around me. It was as if someone had pressed the mute button; the jabber of the gathering priests and the noise of the passing street traffic abruptly ended. I looked at Eph, whose voice was the only thing I could hear. Looking around, I saw others gesturing and talking, but heard nothing. I must be dying or having a stroke, I thought.

"Rip, Monday, what are you doing on Monday?"

"Sleeping, I suppose…it's Easter Monday; did you forget?" I still couldn't hear any of the talking going on around us. I rubbed my eyes, as if the contact would awaken me from a dream, and added, "I'll bite, why—what's up?"

"I'm having a Mass for healing of the sick, and I could use your help."

Somehow, I knew Eph's words were exactly what I needed to hear at that precise moment. I enjoyed celebrating Mass with other priests because it connected me to the image of the first apostles gathering in the upper room. I loved celebrating Mass with anyone at any time whether at church, at home, at nursing homes, at youth groups or at services for schoolchildren; when I was behind the altar, I was content.

Through all of the turmoil and mess I was making of my priesthood, Mass was my salvation. I loved all the subtle movements and prayers of the priest at the altar. When I would hold my hands over the bread and wine and invoke the almighty Spirit of God to change them into His Body and Blood—it did something to me. When I read the Eucharistic Prayer and held the Host in my hands—I was actually holding Jesus. When I would take the chalice and stare inside at the wine, sometimes I'd catch my reflection in what was becoming the Blood of Christ. Holy Eucharist was the only thing keeping me alive. I could never imagine being unable to confect Holy Eucharist. It was in my marrow.

I would be concelebrating with Eph at a healing Mass, one that might radiate some healing over me as well. How could I resist? "What time do you need me?"

"Seven o'clock," he said, and smiled a crooked grin.

The noise around me suddenly returned, which I found puzzling and mysterious. Again, the clamor of the gathering crowd of priests filled the air; I heard the traffic and bits of conversation and the master of ceremonies who was attempting to quiet everyone.

"Fathers, may I have your attention?" the priest hollered above the jabber.

I leaned over to Eph, saying, "There's a job I'd love, lining priests up to walk into a cathedral." Following all the instructions, I whispered to Eph, "Don't forget to exchange the sign of peace with a manly handshake."

"And Fathers, please only use a handshake at the sign of peace," the Master of Ceremonies said, right on cue.

Ephraim looked at me and winked. Then the jostling for position began. The directions concluded and the stream of graying, balding, and limping men, wearing battered white polyester chasubles with flowers, began to move up the sidewalk and into the rear nave of the cathedral.

Back at Holy Cross, the Easter Triduum was rather uneventful. Ron was a liturgical minimalist whose philosophy was a get in and get out as soon as possible. Holy Thursday Mass was about 45 minutes long and on Good Friday we seemed to rush through every prayer, movement and silent moment of remembrance. On Holy Saturday, people brought food for their Easter meal to the church for a priestly blessing, a duty assigned to me. Decorated baskets of meats, eggs, breads, and candies were lined up on the red-carpeted step in the sanctuary; there was even a cake of butter in the shape of a lamb holding a cross.

At sundown, we began the ceremony for the highest Holy Day of our faith—the Great Easter Vigil. Oddly enough, Ron and I began the event standing next to a hibachi grill at the entrance of the church. I held the Paschal Candle and Ron struck a match, lit the fire and said the prayer. The unique aroma of incense mixed with lighter fluid filled the air. I stared at the pitiful little fire before me, wondering if my life would always center on hibachis and butter in the shape of a lamb.

I lit the Paschal Candle, held it high and chanted, "Christ our Light."

The choir and people sang a weak response, "Thanks be to God."

I lowered the candle so that the servers could light their tapers and pass the flame on from person to person. I slowly walked forward and sensed the irony of the moment: the darkest person in the church was holding the Paschal Candle. I stopped midway down the aisle, held the candle high and chanted, "Christ our Light."

"Thanks be to God," the voices responded now growing louder. They must finally be remembering the responsorial song, I thought.

The church was starting to glow orange. I stood at the front, turned and held the candle high and said again, "Christ our Light."

"Thanks be to God."

By Easter Monday, I was exhausted. Ron and I had performed a combined total of 11 services in three days. On top of that, my sister Claudia's family and my father stayed at the rectory for the Easter weekend. After Claudia left for her home back in New Jersey, Dad and I grabbed a hot dog and root beer at a nearby diner. Following lunch, he dropped me back at the rectory and headed home. I sat on the back porch stoop, passing the time with a pinch of snuff and then remembered—it was my birthday.

Eventually I walked across the empty parking lot and into the church. The aroma of incense and Easter lilies still lingered, transporting me back to the many Easters of my life. I slid my hooded alb from a hanger in the sacristy closet, pulled out a white stole from a drawer and jumped in my truck to meet Eph for another healing service.

I had never been to Ephraim's parish, so I left early enough to allow some extra time. When I arrived at Our Lady of Mercy Church, the parking lots and side streets were already full. I maneuvered the truck into a spot on the sidewalk near what I assumed was the rectory and followed a crowd of people going in the side entrance of the church.

Passing through the doors, dipping my right hand in the holy water font and making the sign of the cross—I stopped dead in my tracks. On the wall in front of me was a framed picture of Our Lady of Guadalupe. *Something must be up*, I thought.

Yet, as surprised as I was at my reaction of seeing the picture, the experience of the Mass astonished me even more. It was totally overwhelming. A few days later Ephraim called, asking, "You alright?"

"Jesus, Eph!" I was still overwhelmed.

"Yeah…it's Jesus," he said with a soft chuckle.

"I mean, I could feel it! My hands and even my feet were… like hurting, you know? And they'd sometimes get burning hot when I'd hold them over someone and pray for them. I didn't even know what to pray. I'd just try to be empty and let God do what He wanted to do."

Eph nodded. "It is pretty neat isn't it?"

"Yeah, you could even feel the ones who were resisting. It was wild! I even lost track of time. How many people were there?"

"About 350."

I continued, still revved up from the experience, "You know what else? I was hearing confessions a couple days ago and there was this person; I held my hands over the top of his head for absolution and he started to fall back and rest in the Spirit! He shook his head, you know like he was trying to startle himself back to reality, and asked me what I just did to him."

"What did you say?"

"I just told him I offered Christ's absolution."

I did not know how to interpret the experience, but then a shade of doubt entered my head. Maybe it would be good to talk about it with someone other than Eph. I needed to know if it was real, or if Eph had gone off the deep end. Only a few weeks had passed since the healing Mass and I realized I was already becoming skeptical. Maybe there was another explanation other than just blind faith.

I tried to talk with my spiritual director a couple times about my experience but he offered little guidance, perhaps because he had not witnessed it or maybe he just did not feel the need to believe that faith could heal. In my mind, Father Stan stopped being my spiritual director the day he set up the meeting at the restaurant where I shared my reasons about not wanting to go to Holy Cross. It had to be someone else.

By mid–summer, I turned to my seminary friend Father Ben Tomison, a holy priest and an experienced psychoanalyst. He was scheduled to give a workshop to a religious community of nuns in our diocese on the same day Eph was celebrating the next healing Mass. The timing was perfect for him to attend with me.

After the Mass, Ben and I headed back to Holy Cross, continuing our discussion until he drove the car into the parking lot and shut off the engine. I looked out across the lot at the parish's summer carnival. I really did not like parish festivals. It had nothing to do with faith and were put on just to make money for the church, with the excuse of getting people together for the sake of community was secondary. It wasn't a tough decision for me to commit the "parochial sin" of the priest not walking through the parish festival.

I turned to face Ben. "So, it's real, huh?"

"Most definitely it is. I've sometimes seen people go into frenzy from the preacher, but Ephraim's not doing that. This is the Holy Spirit and it is very powerful. And, it is very hard on the one who has the gift."

That night as parishioners danced to polka music at the festival, I lay in bed and noticed how the streetlight lit up the face of The Virgin of Guadalupe in the picture hanging on the wall.

Hail Mary…

Love *and* Leaving

1997

*"The kingdom of heaven is like a treasure buried in a field, which a
person finds and hides again, and out of joy goes and sells all that he has
and buys that field."*
—from the Gospel of Jesus Christ according to Matthew.

CHAPTER XXI

"Community Care, may I help you?"

"Yes, this is Father Michael Ripple. May I please speak with Wendy Walker?"

"One moment please."

Community Care? Maybe it's a hospital or some sort of social service agency, I thought. I really had no idea since I was returning a call. The phone clicked. "She'll be with you in just a minute; she's finishing up with a patient."

I waited on hold. It must be a hospital or clinic, and she must be a nurse or a nurse's aide, I continued to muse. I had received the pink message as part of my typical morning routine: After Mass, grab a coffee from the kitchen where the housekeeper and two secretaries would be sitting at the table; then, make my way up the shag–carpeted stairs to my second floor office. On the way, I would retrieve any messages placed on the first or second step, which served as my "mailbox" for messages, mail and all other important paperwork.

Suddenly, a female voice came on the telephone: "Hello, this is Dr. Walker."

"Hello, this is Father Michael. I, I...didn't know you were a doctor."

She did not respond to my comment, obviously aware that she was a doctor. "Father, I'd like to make an appointment to see you."

"Are you bleeding?"

"Well, no...bleeding?" she asked.

"I'm sorry, that's just how I ask if it is an emergency and we need to get together as soon as possible." Again, she ignored my inability to carry on an intelligent phone conversation.

"No, I'm not bleeding. I've just been reading this book and I have some questions."

"What is it, what have you been reading?" I asked.

"The Catechism of the Roman Catholic Church."

Crap, I thought, I never read the whole thing. Out loud, I continued, "Whoa, now that's a book!"

"I have some questions and want to talk about them. Would you be willing?"

How was I going to discuss a book with someone as smart as a doctor? Better yet, how was I going to discuss a book I hadn't read? "What does your schedule look like?" I asked.

"I'm off on Wednesdays."

"That will work; how about 10 o'clock next week?"

"That would be fine. Thank you, Father."

"See you then, doctor."

After I hung up, I went downstairs to my room, let Jeb outside, put in a chew of snuff, turned on some George Winston music and opened the book, *The Catechism of the Roman Catholic Church*.

Doctor Wendy Walker arrived at the appointed time the following week. I motioned for her to have a seat in one of the two chairs that sat opposite my desk. I angled the one next to hers and sat down. She had many questions. "I'm not sure about confession. I mean, why can't I just tell my sins directly to God? Why do I need to tell them to a priest?"

"I guess before we answer that, we need to talk about what sin is." And so it began.

As the months wore on, Dr. Walker, who wanted me to call her Wendy, began to attend daily Mass. She had not practiced her Catholic faith for some time. Wendy would park her white Oldsmobile coupe at the end of the parking lot, facing it out so she would be able to leave early and make it on time for work. Every morning from my bedroom window I would look for it. When it wasn't there, I wondered where she was and what she was doing. I knew she was married and I wondered why I never saw her husband with her at Mass on Sundays. I would stand at my window wondering about this woman and her life, daydreaming until Jeb whimpered; it was his way of reminding me I had to let him out.

Every time we met, Wendy was clearly in charge of the conversation. She arrived with an agenda, ranging from questions on birth control to sacraments. Whenever we entered the realm of moral theology or medical ethics, I would cringe inside, fearful that I would not be able to offer significant insights. All I remembered from seminary was no abortion, no euthanasia, and give them nutrition and hydration.

Despite my misgivings, I did share a painful lesson with Wendy that I had learned about medical ethics while at St. Pete's. The doctor from a nearby nursing home had called the rectory out of desperation, wanting me to persuade family members not to remove a feeding tube from their mother. Sadly, there was nothing I could do; the family held firmly to its decision. I didn't need to present the Church's stance—my collar had already done that—but I talked instead about the pain of starvation. Sensing no hope for change, I left the cold vending room where we had met to anoint and pray with the mother. She could not talk, but she squeezed my hand and looked me straight in the eyes—pleading. That was the day I put a face on medical ethics; that was the day I cried for a stranger.

Wendy and I had many such discussions. She would ask the questions and I would do my best to answer. I realized that God wanted her and was calling her into a deeper relationship. I was also inspired by her desire to know and understand her faith. It awakened me. Each question served as another opportunity to delve into her relationship with God. I was witnessing a soul that was being pursued by Him. Her call to holiness was so pure and so honest.

Part of me was jealous. Wendy was married and now she had God loving her and wanting her. I had no person to love; I wasn't sure if God even wanted me.

As autumn and winter wore on, I continued to disregard a growing feeling for a remarkable woman; Wendy was slowly capturing my heart. I had only one option and that was to deny my feelings, reminding myself constantly that she was married—and so was I; there was no way I was going to make that mistake again.

Instead, at night I would fall asleep denying my heart...as the television blared overhead.

CHAPTER XXII

The communion hymn finished and I stood up to do the closing prayer. "I invite all mothers, grandmothers, and mothers–to–be to stand for our Mother's Day Blessing." A scattering of women stood, some proud, some after being coaxed, some young and some old.

I looked out at the congregation and felt an inpouring of grief overtake my heart—I missed my mom. My first Mass as an altar boy was on Mother's Day. I remember looking out into the congregation that day and seeing my mom smiling back at me. Every time I looked, she was looking back at me, her smile making me feel secure and happy. She had seen my first Mass as an altar boy, but never as a priest.

Following Mass, I deposited the Sunday collection bags in the outside night deposit vault at the bank. I returned to the rectory and hopped on my bicycle for a little exercise. Eventually, I met up with members of a cycling group from the parish. We turned a bend and began to climb a hill. I noticed another cyclist coming toward us, who the others recognized and hollered to get her to stop.

It was Wendy, heading out to check on the construction of her new house. She invited us all to bike along with her.

I had seen Wendy a few days earlier at one of our meetings and she shared the news that she had been accepted to the Masters in Theology program at a city university. When I asked about her husband's reaction, Wendy revealed that they planned to divorce. I was surprised. She explained the split would be amicable; they were friends who were no longer in love and had few interests in common. Days later, I was still having trouble imagining a man crazy enough not to be in love with Dr. Wendy Walker.

By the time I finished replaying the conversation in my head, we had reached her half–built house, where she excitedly led us from one imaginary room to another. "Of course, I'll have to buy everything. I don't own a thing," she said.

I couldn't imagine owning a house, let alone building and furnishing one. But this was what Wendy said she wanted. Her brother, sister and her sister's boyfriend would also be moving in and living with her. It sounded like an episode from the television show, Friends.

Wendy had a new home, new friends and a recently–awakened faith. She seemed so happy. Did that mean her marriage was that awful? Was she as unfulfilled in her marriage as I had become as a priest?

Over the next few weeks, our lives continued to connect. I quickly came to know Wendy's daily schedule. She had separated from her husband and was now living with her aunt just a few minutes from the parish. When I would pass by and see her white

Oldsmobile, my heart would do a little flutter. I just wanted to be with her.

One morning, I looked out of the rectory window and saw Wendy's car parked for morning Mass. I hurried to leave a note on the windshield: Dinner tonight, Mexican food? To celebrate your acceptance to the master's program and our trip to Honduras?— Michael.

These seemed like good reasons to meet. We had decided to visit my old friend John at his mission in Honduras. The plan was for us to do mission work with him and the idea had come after a healing Mass we attended together. Afterwards, we sat in Eph's rectory and I talked about wanting to visit John. Wendy had said she liked the idea. Admittedly, we didn't need to eat at a Mexican restaurant to chat about it, but I was looking for any reason to spend time with her.

That night, after dinner, we visited Wendy's doctor and nurse friends at the hospital, followed by a stroll through her old college grounds. On our way home we stopped by a cemetery that was along one of our bicycling roads—making our time together last a little longer. We jumped the old split rail fence and lay in the grass, watching the fireflies perform a carefully choreographed light show.

In the distance, lightning flashed from cloud to cloud, illuminating the shadowy, dark storm clouds. We lay on the ground and waited for the storm to move directly overhead. The sides of our head touched, and I felt an electric charge jolt through me. I wanted to blurt out—*what was that, did you feel that?*

Thunder boomed and the rains soon followed. We ran back to the car, soaking wet, laughing like children. I drove us back to the rectory. Wendy got out and came around to the driver's side and with a quick hug, she was back in her car and gone.

I fell asleep thanking God for such a good friend and feeling that maybe we had purposely been brought together. A couple of days later I called Wendy. "What are you doing?"

"Oh, I was buying some lamps for the house, and now I'm thinking about going to see a movie but my aunt and grandmother say I really shouldn't go out alone."

It was an opportunity to spend more time with her. "I'll go with you."

"Really?"

"Sure. I'll pick you up. But first I'll need to drop off some food vouchers for someone who needs some help."

It was a great evening. We saw the movie and I didn't feel the least bit uncomfortable. I felt as though I had spent the evening with a special friend, someone I wouldn't mind being around for a very long time, perhaps for life. Afterwards, we shared a big plate of fries at Denny's and then headed back.

When we were less than a mile from where she was staying, I turned and said, "You know...when our eyes meet, I feel like our hearts connect." Mine jumped. Oh, no, had I really said that? She glanced at me, then turned and looked out the passenger window quietly acknowledging me with a nod—and a "Hmm."

I turned the truck onto her street. "Here we are."

She didn't say a word and hopped out of the truck before I could get around to open her door. "Bye." She smiled and headed through the open garage door.

"See you later," I said, feeling awkward, standing in front of the headlights. She turned and waved.

Back at the rectory, I fought the urge to call her to explain the words and the meaning behind them. I had meant so much more than the words conveyed. I didn't want to force it. I wanted to explain that my heart had been changed forever because of her, and that I wanted her to be in my life—no matter what path I followed.

I needed to let Wendy know how I felt, because there was something she didn't know; I was getting ready to leave Holy Cross and maybe even the priesthood—maybe even because of her.

CHAPTER XXIII

Five years into priesthood, I again traveled north across the border and into Pennsylvania to meet my classmates. It was a time to relax, enjoy some camaraderie and suppress any dark truths lurking in our hearts. This year's reunion took place in Gettysburg.

I took my bicycle along, hoping some solitude on the road would give me much needed time to exercise, think and pray. On the second day, I arose early and took a 15–mile ride south back into Maryland. By the time the midmorning sun was heating up the day, I was standing at the base of the giant gold statue of Mary situated on the mountain hillside just outside of Emmitsburg.

I took a sip from my water bottle, sat down on a concrete curb and began to pray. "I'm a mess. I have no control over my life. I mean, I gave it to You but, well—I mean all I ever wanted was You. What happened? I can't keep living this way. Maybe I'm just not meant to be a priest."

Looking up at the statue I added a desperate, "Mary, help me!"

Later, I stood alone at a clump of trees, in the middle of the Gettysburg battlefield. The timing of my visit was near the very hour of Pickett's Charge—the fatal surge of Confederate men and spirit long ago—that had saturated the soil beneath my feet with the blood of thousands. It was known as the High Tide of the Confederacy.

The quiet was interrupted only by the sound of insects in the tall grasses and the rustling of leaves jostled about by a hot midday summer breeze. A haze seemed to rise before me from out of the brown dry fields. Several tourists walked nearby. I fixed my gaze on the vast open space, which had once separated the Confederate and Union armies.

I knew the layout of the land and the story of the battle all too well. I had walked, hiked and ridden through the surrounding battlefields and woods at least 100 times in all seasons. I knew this place, the history and the stories like the back of my hand. However, today my mind was not on the land or the battle. I was in my own battle; I was spiritually paralyzed.

The sun was burning the top of my head. I twisted my hair back into a ponytail, closed my eyes, stared blankly ahead and felt the nothingness within me. A warm breeze touched my skin, giving me goose bumps, and a bead of sweat ran down the middle of my back. I felt a deep physical pain in my chest, like a knife piercing my soul.

I knew God was here.

He found me, just as He found Adam after he took a bite of the apple. I felt ashamed. My knees grew weak and I thought I might faint. Walking further into the field, I sat down, held my head in my hands and stared at the ground just inches from my face. Shaking my head, I whispered, "I can't do it. I can't keep living this way. My God! What am I going to do? I've screwed up my life so badly! I've sinned and I've hurt people. God, forgive me. What am I going to do?"

I don't know how long I sat in the same spot. After a while I grew very tired and lay back in the grass—in the same place those poor soldiers had fallen. I closed my eyes, poured out my heart and retraced my life. Like a flourish of fireworks, memories of moments with God flashed through my mind: my first Holy Communion as a boy, my desire for union with Christ as a young man and my first Mass as a priest. The memories also included my sins. I gave everything to God—pouring tears into the dry soil.

I thought about how even as a young child I had wanted to be married to Christ just like the saints in the stories I read. It never fully happened and I assumed it was because my sin had always gotten in the way.

Part of me wanted to die on this field stained by death; yet a greater part of me wanted to live. I was coming to grips with the fact that I could no longer live as a priest. I had failed and sinned, and I did not fit in. All I could point to in my life were my failures and sins. I had no love. Was I even meant to love?

And then, her image came into my mind—Wendy.

There is the spiritual maxim that good and evil coexist simultaneously in our lives. With the gift of free will, God empowers us to choose between the two. In the midst of my despair there in that field, I chose life and love. The love I chose was for this woman, who had no idea what was happening to me.

For months, Wendy had talked with me about her religious beliefs, while I had been listening—and falling in love with her. Maybe there was a reason we had met. Perhaps God, who had found me in the garden, ashamed and full of sin, had decided not to cast me out; maybe He was willing to try again to regain my soul.

That evening, my classmates and I celebrated Holy Mass on a makeshift altar in my hotel room. On a low dresser along the wall, we placed a square white cloth beneath a ceramic chalice, patent and crucifix, and a burning white vigil candle.

I held the Host in my hands, bowed down and prayed aloud, "Take this all of you and eat; this is my Body which is given up for you; do this in remembrance of me."

I raised the Host higher, noticing the reflection of the five of us in the mirror on the wall. I knew this would be the last Mass I would celebrate with them.

CHAPTER XXIV

After the reunion, I returned to the parish with new insight and resolution. I had no sense of what to do next or where to seek guidance. There was no one at the parish I could trust.

Would it be logical to talk to Wendy about it? Of course, she had no idea what had been going on inside of me. Aside from sharing complaints about parish life, I usually only talked with Wendy about spirituality and the quest for holiness—which was exactly why I was so taken by her. I felt it wouldn't be fair to spring this on her, at least not yet.

For one week, I waited, suffering a form of confusion paralysis.

Though I had contemplated leaving parish life, and possibly even the diocese, I had not considered leaving the priesthood, at least not seriously enough to delve into the process. This was a reality I hadn't expected to face. I knew priests took what was termed a leave of absence from the active ministry. Over the years, I had seen the announcements posted by the diocesan personnel office in the weekly diocesan newspaper stating that Father So–and–So was taking a six–month leave of absence.

The implication was that the individual was using that time to decide whether to continue as a parish priest. It was rare, however, for a priest to return after a leave; to my way of thinking, a 'leave' was another term for…gone.

Wendy knew me as her priest friend. I kept wondering if she would have anything to do with me if I told her everything. For one week, I labored over the fact that I had fallen in love with a woman who had no reason to think I was leaving the priesthood and no reason to think my decision was based in large part on my love for her.

How would I tell her?

The question played in my head and heart for days. What about my soul? Am I jeopardizing it by leaving or has the damage already been done by my failure as a priest? Was leaving now the right thing to do in order to save my soul?

I felt like I was playing a part in Franco Zeffirelli's film about St. Francis of Assisi, titled, *Brother Sun, Sister Moon.* In a memorable scene, Francis finds one of his followers kneeling along the side of a narrow cobblestone alley, soaked from the rain and praying aloud, "God have mercy on me a sinner! God have mercy on me a sinner! God have mercy on me a sinner!" Francis approaches, embraces him and says, "I think God heard you the first time." The distraught man confesses he cannot live the austere life that was required by Francis and his community. That was my story, summed up in a single scene and I prayed that God would have mercy on me.

I took a day off to clear my head and drove out to visit Father John, who was getting ready to travel back to Central America. We both made the drive back to my parish, where we planned to meet with Wendy over dinner to discuss our upcoming trip to the orphanage. He was reading aloud from my Spanish dictionary.

"Dame un beso," John said, which means "Give me a kiss."

"Do you use that one at the monastery?"

"Nice," he said, giving a caustic smile.

We arrived at Wendy's house, and she met us in the driveway. "Dame un beso," I said without thinking.

She tilted her head, smiled at John, and asked, "Should we take my car? There's more room."

Throughout dinner and during our return drive to St. Francis, we continued to plan our mission trip. I pulled Wendy's car alongside the monastery entrance, and John hopped out. It would be the last time we would see him until the trip.

"See you guys in two months!" He slammed the passenger door, and we watched him cross the footbridge and disappear into the monastery. I slowly pulled the car around and headed out.

"That's St. Anthony Hall," I said, pointing to my right. "That's where I lived for five years. And over there is the Basilica."

Its worn red brick reflected the pink and orange glow from the lights in the parking lot. "Want to see if any of the buildings are open?"

"Really, this late? Don't they lock it up?" Wendy asked, with a yawn.

We crossed the parking lot and found that the seminary building was open. Together we walked through the dark hallways, lit only by green and red exit signs. I showed her my old rooms and the chapel. Once outside, we sat on the concrete and brick banisters of the front porch.

"This is where I'd sometimes hang out while skipping a class; and right here are the flowers that I peed on because I didn't like the friar who planted them. I know it was adolescent and passive–aggressive…but it felt good."

She cracked a smile, although her look showed a hint of motherly disapproval. I started to feel uneasy and embarrassed after sharing the 'watering' story. I needed to be serious. This was my chance to change the level of conversation and possibly tell her what was going on in my life. I had so much I wanted to say. I wanted to tell her how I valued her friendship, and how I viewed it as a gift from God. I wanted to share with her what was going on inside me about the priesthood. Most of all, I wanted to share— that I had fallen in love with her.

Instead, I babbled on.

On the drive back to the diocese, I drove and Wendy fell asleep. Occasionally I would catch a glimpse of her when headlights would shine through the windshield. Hours later, I pulled into the rectory parking lot. "Do you want to hang out in the back yard for a while?" I asked. "It's a pretty clear night for stars."

"Sure, why not?" she said, smiling.

Thank God, I thought. I hadn't bored her to death; she still wants to hang with me.

"I'm off tomorrow," she said, and looked at her watch and smiled a slight smile. "I mean today. I'll catch up on sleep later today."

In the backyard of the rectory, we spread a blanket, then lay down and gazed at the stars. Of course, I continued to babble without saying anything meaningful.

"Oh my gosh!" she yelled, pointing her finger toward the sky. "Did you see that? It was a shooting star, wasn't it?"

We had brought my dog Jeb along, and he was busy patrolling the perimeter of the yard. We were busy pointing and counting the stars streaking across the sky. I kept talking about spiritual friendship, saying not all spiritual friends are meant to be married; some may just be friends forever.

Wendy rolled onto her side, grabbed my left arm and with a voice a bit hoarse and sleepy, whispered, "If this is friendship, then it can't get much better."

My heart fluttered.

At five in the morning, we gathered a few more blankets from her home and along with Jeb, headed to a camp her dad owned just outside of Hagerstown, Maryland, a drive of about two hours. I wanted to leave before the housekeeper, secretaries and the pastor arrived for the day and witnessed the assistant priest asleep in the backyard with a soon-to-be-divorced woman, both guarded by his trusty Labrador.

At camp, we spread the blankets on a patch of grass and crashed. Jeb kept busy bringing us sticks, limbs and anything that wasn't attached, laying them around us. We both slept. The sun crept higher and higher in the sky. I was enjoying the present moment with Wendy, not thinking or worrying about anything, feeling as if the past and future had collided on the blanket and no longer existed.

At one point, I awoke, leaned on my side, propped my head up with my hand and just stared at Wendy. It was so clear. My true love has been in my life for the past year. She opened her eyes and squinted from the sunlight. She caught me gazing at her.

"What are you thinking?" she whispered.

"I'm thinking I need to tell you something."

"What?"

"Well, you know…I've…" I felt my heart beating against my chest. "I've fallen in love with you."

To my surprise and utter amazement, Wendy opened her arms and reached for me saying, "I love you too, Michael."

We moved inside the cabin and again fell asleep, this time while holding each other. I felt her heartbeat, her breath, her body—I felt her love. It was the most peaceful sleep I had experienced in years.

When we awoke, Wendy looked at me for a long time before saying, "Michael, I'm afraid."

My heart did a leap in the moment of reality. "Me too."

The fear was settling in for both of us. Was it a foreshadowing? Would we now suffer the repercussions of loving each other?

Was this feeling of love going to cause Wendy only pain and suffering? She had just started on her journey back to the Church and God; in spite of my love for her, I didn't want to be the obstacle that would prevent her from uniting with Christ. Just hours ago we had felt hope and possibility. Now the hope was being quickly diminished by an overwhelming sense of dread and fear. True love was terrifying us and if that wasn't enough, we soon had to go back to the real world and face the reality of that love.

We didn't have the luxury of riding off into the sunset.

The inevitable arrival back to reality was prolonged with an impromptu stop at a nearby state park lake. I made my way down the steep, rusty steps to the boat dock and Wendy stayed behind. "I need to call my sister; the signal is pretty weak down by the water. You go ahead," she said, and dialed her cell phone.

I stood on the dock, watching the twilight reflect on the waves, filled with a mixture of utter joy and frightening apprehension. Behind me in the parking lot I heard Wendy laughing. She made her way down to the dock and sat down beside me. "She was mad."

"Christine?" I asked. I flipped off my sandals and touched my toes in the water. "Why?"

"She was angry, but just because she didn't know where I was. She figured that I was somewhere with you."

"So what did you tell her?"

"I told her where we were and then she asked if you professed your undying love for me and I said—Yes! Then she said, 'Well, he can't have his cake and eat it too!' "

If only it were as easy as giving up cake.

I knew all too well what would happen next. I was thankful that I wouldn't have to face it alone. For now though, we still had a few hours. Wendy laid her head on my lap and soon fell asleep. I leaned over and gave her a gentle kiss on the forehead.

My next kiss would be when I reverenced the altar at Mass and said, "In the name of the Father, the Son, and the Holy Spirit."

CHAPTER XXV

I sat on the small concrete stoop by the back door of the rectory and watched Jeb give chase to some chipmunks near the woodpile as I sipped coffee. Beside me lay a green book entitled The Code of Canon Law. Half of it was written in Latin, the official language of the Roman Catholic Church; the other half was in English—thankfully. I began leafing through the pages in a desperate search to find a way out of the priesthood that would be acceptable for both of us.

I was surprised at how I felt at this moment. Here I was deciding to leave everything I'd lived for since the day I received my first Holy Communion; strangely, I was in total peace. I opened the book of Canon Law and set myself to the task.

Over the years listening to others talk I remembered hearing that a priest could be released from the vow of celibacy when he was 40, or after he had been out of the ministry for five years. What about the possibility of having children? I did the math; I would be 38, Wendy 35, before we could start a family. "That's crazy," I mumbled as I continued my search.

Canon 290 Loss of the Clerical State: "After it has been validly received, sacred ordination never becomes invalid; a cleric, however, loses the clerical state...." I moved my finger down the page to Canon 291: "Loss of the clerical state does not entail a dispensation from the obligation of celibacy, which is granted by the Roman Pontiff alone."

What? Would I really need a note from the Pope? What are the chances of that happening?

In my head I penned my official letter: Dear Pope John Paul, I thought I was called by God to become a priest, because I wanted more than ever to be united to Jesus Christ. But it just hasn't worked out. I have fallen in love with someone and I want to get married. May I have your permission?

I had no desire or intention of asking the Church for permission. At that moment, I felt that the Church had failed me.

I kept reading and found Canon 1394, which essentially states that a cleric who attempts even a civil marriage incurs an automatic suspension. I slammed the book down beside me on the concrete. The Canons clearly spelled out the rules, but I didn't want to play the game anymore. I decided to make an immediate break.

I knew God loved Wendy and I, and believed the love we shared was a gift. I also knew God would provide a way for us and not abandon us. In my search for truth, I had found love and was certain our souls would survive somehow, someway, someday. If our love and my actions were considered to be sinful, I prayed the consequences would fall on me and not on her.

One night when we fell asleep in each other's arms, we both awoke at the same moment and looked into each other's eyes. "I promise to love you and honor you," I said, and stroked her hair.

She smiled and whispered, "In sickness and in health, in good and bad."

"I will be your husband, forever."

"And I will be your wife, forever."

I had heard those vows exchanged many times, yet I would not be allowed to speak them in the church I served. We would never be able to marry in the Church, which now considered us consigned on the path to damnation.

My faith and belief in marriage could not console me as I considered my suspension from the Roman Catholic Church. I believed that marriage was a sacrament through which a husband and wife grew not only in love, but also in holiness. Marriage was a visible union of man and woman, as well as a union of the two with their God. I believed the new life born out of marriage was a gift as was parenthood. The facts were clear; we could never again be part of the Roman Catholic Church.

I decided to make an immediate break. The question was, how immediate? Would it take days or weeks? Wendy said she was willing to wait 'forever'. For a week, we lived in limbo. We spent every evening together trying to plan our future—from my job to our wedding. We would drive miles out of the diocese just to have dinner, where nobody would recognize us. We would hold hands, pray the rosary and try to come up with the best possible way for me to leave, and for us to begin our life together. However, there was no easy 'way'.

One thing was sure in our minds; we both needed support from our family. It was time for me to make the drive home and share the news with my father.

Dad sat on the wrought iron chair and traced the decorative leaves of the armrest with his index finger. I perched nervously on the brick banister leaning my back against the pillar, watching the traffic in the distance on the interstate. I figured he was going to say one of two things: Michael, this is too fast; or, what are you going to do for a job? Maybe he would say both.

Dad cleared his throat and spoke, "You know what my sister, your Aunt Geraldine, said to me that day we were visiting you at the rectory?"

"No, what?" I remembered the visit at the beginning of summer. His sister had come from Cleveland for a few days. The two took a holiday, traveling around with their younger sister, visiting their old homes and putting flowers at cemeteries.

"It was when Wendy stopped by to give you some photographs from the bike trip," Dad continued. "In the car on the way home, Geraldine said to me, 'She's the one; she has eyes for Michael.'"

I immediately felt Dad's support and love. "Michael, you've been leaving for the past five years," he said, smiling and looking directly at me.

Seeing his smile made me feel so relieved. I no longer felt I was letting him down. And though he knew little of what had been going on in my life—he didn't need to. He didn't need me to be a priest because he loved me for who I was. The two of us drove over to Wendy's medical practice, where he gave her a big hug, and joked about his being too old for all this excitement. Wendy placed her stethoscope over his heart. "Nope, you're fine! You've got a good ticker," she joked.

Later that day, I called from the rectory to set an appointment with the auxiliary bishop. I looked out over the parking lot and dialed the phone. Volunteers were erecting tents for the parish summer festival. I remembered sitting in the parking lot a year ago during festival time, with Father Ben talking about the Healing Masses. I smiled, thinking that I may also have been "healed" at that service.

Over the receiver the bishop's secretary said, "The earliest the bishop has available is next Wednesday."

"That's fine, thank you."

Hanging up the phone, I felt as if I had already left. I wondered if the bishop would even be surprised at my decision. I decided to call Wendy at work. It had only been a couple of hours since Dad and I left her office, but I wanted to make sure she was ready for all of this. Maybe I had to reassure myself that we were both ready.

"Are you sure? I mean, about all this, Michael? I'm so nervous."

My throat tightened as I said to her, "Yes, Wendy, why? We knew this wasn't going to be easy." I tried my best to assure her, a little surprised at her sudden indecisiveness.

"I know; I'm just afraid, for you," her voice was tender and soft.

I felt her love for me and realized I had never given or received love like this before. "And, I'm worried about you," I said.

I hoped I would be able to protect us from the inevitable repercussions of my decision. I couldn't leave fast enough. I had at least two more weekends to act as if nothing had changed.

During Sunday Mass, I caught Wendy staring at my feet, as I sat in the priest's chair in the sanctuary next to the altar. As the cantor sang the responsorial psalm. I wiggled my toes in my sandals, hoping to break Wendy of her stare. She seemed so far away. I caught her eyes and as she looked up and smiled, they were filled with tears.

We had worked out a code to help keep one another from becoming too distraught during Mass and other public moments. When I folded my hands and placed my two index fingers against my lips—that was a kiss; when I folded my arms—that was a hug. We had only a few more days to live like this, but it seemed an eternity.

At the Chancery, there was an office for everything. Priests can get help with just about every aspect of life, as it pertains to parish ministry. There were offices for parish schools and education, stewardship, youth ministry, insurance and continuing education. They even had an office for athletics. There was a vocation director, but no one to help with the transition out of a vocation. There was no office, no safe haven, for a man simply wanting to talk with someone about transitioning out of the priesthood, someone not quite as determined as a bishop.

If I chose to resign, I would have no paycheck, no insurance and no place to live. As a result, though I had no plans to return, I felt compelled to maintain the charade and told the bishop I was taking a leave of absence. I needed to keep health insurance. The bishop leaned back and asked, "Mike, have you received counseling?"

I did not feel obliged to explain my feelings or discuss my counseling with a man whom I felt had so ignored me over the past two years. I would never again leave myself so open and I had no intentions of baring my soul today. I had lost trust in all the people and mechanisms of the system, which had failed me. I felt lucky to have the love of God and the gift of God's love in and through Wendy, a love I was certain had saved me. Thus, in my mind, it was over.

"Yes, Bishop, I have been receiving counseling since my first year of priesthood. I responded."

The bishop's only request of me was to leave without a word, ostensibly 'under the guise of night.' I was to say nothing to the parishioners. I was to say nothing from the pulpit; just pack up and leave. To this last request, I was obedient. It seemed the best way to avoid bringing any added attention to Wendy and her family. Later that week after I celebrated my last Mass at the parish, I packed my pickup and moved in with Wendy, exhausted, exhilarated and now an official 'ex–priest.'

It was truly over.

Becoming *a* husband, *a* father *and an* Episcopalian

1997–2000

"Blessed be the Lord, who has shown me
A wondrous love…"
—from the Book of Psalms.

CHAPTER XXVI

An old metal oscillating fan barely stirred the stuffy humid air in the county marriage license bureau, slowly circulating a smell best described as essence of old library. A florescent light flickered above us, as we stood before a woman seated at the desk.

The clerk adjusted her glasses and gave a cursory glance over them at the two of us. We stood there silently at the whim of a public employee waiting to know if she deemed us worthy to receive a marriage license. She looked at the date stamped on Wendy's divorce decree and said with a chuckle, "Boy, the two of you don't waste any time do you?"

I glanced at Wendy, raised my eyebrows and forced a smile. I looked around to see if there was anyone around that I knew. Though I had performed dozens of marriages now recorded through this office, I felt naked and paranoid—and with just cause.

The previous evening while Wendy and I stood at a deli counter, I noticed a woman tugging at her husband's arm and pointing at us, then cupping her hand over his ear and whispering. Others even took the time to locate my new address so they could send us hate mail, which I made sure I intercepted before Wendy could see the spiteful letters. One self–appointed priest paparazzi took the time and energy to untie garbage bags left on the curb for pickup in order to look through our trash.

The marriage license lady coughed a rough smoker's hack, pointed to the paper and said, "On this line put down the total years of education between the two of you."

The answer to that question involved over two–thirds of our collective age, not to mention hundreds of thousands of dollars of debt. We made a joke about it, filled out the forms and left the office with a license. At least we would be legal in the eyes of the government.

We were married several weeks later by a Justice of the Peace in a civil ceremony void of the mention of God, Jesus Christ or the Holy Spirit. Our honeymoon lasted a mere 48 hours at a resort in southwestern Pennsylvania.

Six months later, we decided to move from Wendy's house. We both wanted a fresh start as a couple in a new place, in a new location—definitely more than two miles from Holy Cross.

A new setting was not only necessary for our sanity—but also for the sake of our expected baby.

CHAPTER XXVII

"Michael, do something!" Wendy screamed. "He's here!"

I lifted the white bed sheet and saw the crest of my son's head.

"Stop! He's here. You gotta stop!" I hollered to the nurses and the doctor.

They were maneuvering Wendy's hospital bed through the doorway of her room to the delivery room. But life wasn't going to happen as planned. They pushed the bed back into the room just in time.

For a moment there was total silence. Then, two cries broke through, first Wendy's cry, and then that of a baby.

"Is he an Isaac?" Wendy asked.

"Yes, he's an Isaac!"

I was barely able to respond, struck mute by the miracle before me. The doctor stretched my son's umbilical cord and directed me to cut it. My fingers, arms, and shoulders went completely numb with pins and needles; the sensation then traveled right to my heart. For a split second, I thought I might have a heart attack and die right in the hospital room, within sight of a son who would never know me. Wendy would have to tell him how his father died at childbirth.

The nurse handed Isaac to Wendy. I watched her hold him on her chest and begin to weep and shake uncontrollably. I cried right along with her. The sight carved a niche in my heart and soul forever. I was witnessing love being born, a love so pure, so unblemished and so perfect. Nothing else would matter now—nothing because I was a father.

I closed my eyes, and tears rolled down my cheeks. I whispered, "Thank you. Thank you, God."

Who would have guessed that Wendy, who had once said she didn't want children, would become a mother? And I, the one who had taken a promise of celibacy would be an actual father? Both of us were now parents.

For the first eight months of Wendy's pregnancy, I didn't want my son to be named after me. Then, a few weeks before he was born, I awoke from a dream in the middle of the night, remembering only a command to name my son Michael. I woke Wendy to tell her my change of heart. She agreed. We would name him Michael Isaac Ripple. He would be called Isaac, which means 'God's laughter.'

In just one year Wendy and I had evolved from parishioner and priest, to acquaintances passing each other on a bicycle ride, to friends, to wife and husband, to mother and father. *In just one year!*

John was back for a couple of weeks from the mission in Honduras. We scheduled Isaac's baptism to coincide with his visit. Father Jerry Lensosky, my first pastor, saw to it that Isaac would be baptized at St. Peter's Church. From that day forward he became known as 'Uncle Jerry.' We gathered around the font, while John struggled to perform the Rite of Baptism in English, having spoken only Spanish for a while. At that moment it didn't matter that I was an ex–priest or that Wendy was divorced. We were all family, saints and sinners. It wasn't about us—it was about Michael Isaac and God.

It never crossed our minds not to have Isaac baptized Roman Catholic.

A few months later we moved 600 miles away and out of the diocese for good. We were finally starting over, and we had a plan. I was to begin studies at the local university with the hopes of attending medical school, and Wendy had already joined a local pediatric practice. We bought a turn–of–the–century red brick house, and began renovating it the day we moved in.

We attended Mass when we chose to, usually every other Sunday. Technically, neither of us was allowed to receive Holy Communion, but we did it anyway. Even as a priest, I had encouraged divorced and remarried parishioners to receive Holy Communion, always feeling that the Church needed to change its old–fashioned rules. Why should anyone reject the Body of Christ for the sake of abiding by what I thought was outdated church thinking? Divorced or remarried, I always believed God wanted to be with us. I now extended that theory to myself as an ex–priest and to my wife. Only later would I know the wrongness of my thinking at that time.

We went to Mass and received the Body of Christ without caring about people judging us. We attended cloaked in anonymity and received the Holy Eucharist because we deemed ourselves worthy. Despite my strong stance, I found it odd that every time I attended Mass—at any church—I felt out of place.

We would alternate between two churches in town; one was extremely liberal in its liturgy, the other stagnant. I could only take the liberal one in small doses because the priest made himself the center of attention. In some ways, it reminded me of what I could have become, and I thanked God for sending Wendy to save me from that fate. The other church was your basic get–in–get–out, with no social or theological agenda. It was the one we chose on this Sunday.

The organist began the opening hymn, and the priest walked from the sacristy to the side aisle. He looked over the congregation and our eyes met—we both smiled. It was a classmate from St. Francis. I had no idea he was in this diocese, let alone at this church. I wondered if he would be uncomfortable with me being at Mass. I was certain he knew what had happened; priest gossip spreads faster than a wildfire on dry brush. Even though I remembered him as being pretty laid back, I started to wonder if we should receive Holy Communion.

My former classmate went on with Mass and I went deeper into my head—engaging in theological battle. Because Wendy and I were not reconciled with God and the Roman Catholic Church, we were not supposed to receive any of the sacraments. I did not agree. My theology taught me that the Body of Christ was given freely to serve as food for our spiritual journey. Still, argue as I might with the voices in my head, the official rules of the church kept talking louder and louder. I decided to pay no heed.

The people filed out of the pews and made their way up the center aisle. I slid off the kneeler and sat on the edge of the pew. I slowly lifted the kneeler and stood up, all the while feeling my head being squeezed by the rapid onset of a tension headache—the way a crown of thorns might feel pushing from the inside out.

We slowly walked up the center aisle towards the Eucharistic minister distributing Communion to our side. As I approached, my classmate looked over at me, held up the Host and said, "My brother Michael, The Body of Christ." I reached out and he placed a piece of the priest's Host in my hand.

The gesture was fraternal, and at first, it made me feel as if I could keep living this way as a secretly–suspended–ex–priest–who–attempted–marriage existence. Soon the thoughts were replaced by more questions, frustrations and anger at what I considered an archaic institution filled with mixed messages.

That Sunday was the last time we went to a Roman Catholic Mass.

CHAPTER XXVIII

A tractor–trailer barreled past with a loud whoosh kicking up road dust and rocking our Ford Expedition. I stood by the opened passenger door holding Wendy as she cried. The car's electronic bell dinged with an annoying cadence. Her crying turned into uncontrollable sobbing; she was having trouble catching her breath.

What had begun as a discussion about work had turned into crying, then coughing, then hyperventilating and now a need for air. I had no idea what to do except to stand there and hold her. I tried to calm her, saying over and over, "Shh…it's okay. It will be okay."

"No, it isn't, Michael!" she wailed.

Cars whizzed by and someone honked their horn. I glanced at the backseat to see Isaac in his car seat. He was awake and pushing buttons on his toy phone. He was so beautiful. I wondered what was going through his two–year–old mind, and I worried about what Wendy was feeling.

I did this to her. That's all I was able to think when our new life seemed to be too much, which at this particular moment—it did. I held her and asked God for his help. I wondered if my actions had brought on this pain and anxiety.

I knew that fatigue was also a key player. Wendy had been working long days and weekends to support us. She was the doctor on call, going in for emergencies several times a week at all hours. Sometimes she would have to call in a medical transport helicopter for a patient. Whenever I would hear the helicopter fly over our house, I'd tell Isaac, "Mommy will be home in half an hour." As if the long hours were not enough, the situation was compounded by the daily injustices of a less–than–desirable office environment. Once happy in her profession, Wendy now disliked going to work.

A pickup truck with huge tires hummed past and honked its horn at us.

Who was I kidding thinking that I could also be a doctor? That was the immediate plan. I would go to medical school, but there was no way I would ever make it—and I knew it. I was barely passing chemistry and anatomy on an undergraduate level.

I had class every day and a lab every other night, and in the few remaining hours, I worked at being a new dad, a new husband, and a son to my father who had been staying with us. In addition, we were trying to renovate our house, a project that demonstrated that my expertise in plumbing, carpentry and electricity matched my academic abilities—nil.

With so many demands on my time, I often felt I wasn't doing anything well; when I was at school, I felt I should be home with my son; when home, I should be working on studies or a home project; when studying or fixing, I should be spending time with Isaac and Wendy. At the end of the day, no matter what I had chosen to accomplish, I felt inept and inadequate.

I knew we had love in our hearts but it couldn't mask all the other issues. In so many aspects of our lives we didn't belong: Wendy didn't belong where she was working. I didn't belong in my academic pursuit; and, we didn't belong to any church or religion. Even worse, we felt trapped by a mortgage, car payments and med school loans.

Wendy caught her breath that day and we returned to the truck and continued on our way. However, the memory of that moment led us in a new direction. We knew life would have to change—again.

We were blessed on so many ways: We had found love, we had a beautiful baby, we enjoyed good health and we wanted for nothing. Still, I couldn't deny that something was missing. Wendy was putting in hours and I was failing at finding a secular vocation. It was as if we were lost in the desert with no peace, seeing the Promised Land but not able to enter it.

Yes, there was much change ahead.

I had to take a realistic look at my dream of becoming a psychiatrist. The journey would require six years of study, with little time for Isaac and Wendy along the way. In reality, Wendy would be a single working mother and I would be married to books, lectures, labs and more debt. I needed to find a shorter road to employment. It wasn't long before I changed my course of studies to graduate clinical psychology, which would be the fastest and easiest way for me to become marketable.

We also needed change in the area of faith. We were ready to put down roots in a faith community after trying to go it alone for two years. We even celebrated Mass in our upstairs prayer room. Our first at–home celebration was with Mike Smitts, my ordination classmate. He and his family made the drive from Ohio to partake in our first illegal Palm Sunday Eucharist in our prayer room.

The prayer room was the first room we renovated. I rough–plastered the walls and ceiling to match, and Wendy placed Isaac's little feet on the wall to make an imprint in the wet joint compound. Choosing a deep earthy clay color, we painted the walls and ceiling and highlighted them with sandy swirls. The effect transported visitors to a cave just off the Mediterranean. Jerry donated a church kneeler, which soon became a favorite spot for Isaac to play. On top of the bookcase filled with theology and spiritual classics was an old sick–call set with a wooden crucifix.

Our Eucharistic celebration with the Smitts began with my Dad stealing palms from the nearby church. We used a ceramic chalice and patent that Wendy had made and given to me as a birthday gift. Isaac and Mike's son fell asleep during our reading of the Passion and prayer offering. Mike and I then concelebrated the Eucharistic Prayer. It was the first time since leaving the priesthood I had invoked the Holy Spirit to change the bread and wine into the Body and Blood of Christ.

Even though the scene hearkened back to the early days of the apostles, it left me wanting more. The Body of Christ, a failed attempt at homemade unleavened bread, tasted like wood; the Blood of Christ, tasted like cheap wine. Something was definitely missing. I just couldn't put my finger on it. Maybe my pride kept me from acknowledging it.

Wendy and I celebrated a few illegal Masses with another couple we had met when we moved to the area, Tim and Mary Beth Saunders. They had twin daughters born one year after Isaac. We met them when we bought a wave runner from their marina and connected from the start as friends, new parents and adults, who were also looking for meaning in life.

One evening, following dinner, the kids fell asleep, and we decided to have Mass. This time, even though the prayer was meaningful, I felt like I was abusing a gift—as if I had said something hurtful to a loved one, then immediately regretted the words. Was I breaking the heart of Jesus by celebrating Mass?

I never shared what I felt with Wendy, because I didn't want her to misinterpret my feelings as regret for leaving the priesthood, but I knew then that I didn't want to continue to pray like this. We needed to put down roots not only for us, but also for Isaac. We needed to be part of some ritual with God, part of a community that believed in the real presence of Jesus Christ in the Bread and Wine.

Changing my course of studies was easy. Our bigger challenge would be finding a church that welcomed us and celebrated Eucharist in a manner that meshed with my lifelong beliefs.

Never did I imagine it would be in an Episcopal church—as an Episcopal priest.

CHAPTER XXIX

I sat alone in the empty church and stared at the red glass container holding the candle that burned next to the tabernacle. "I don't know what to do," I whispered to myself. "I never fit in the Church as a priest and now we can't fit in as a couple."

I looked up at the crucifix and closed my eyes.

I didn't have much time to stay. Isaac would be waking from his nap, and, even though my Dad was watching him, I felt guilty if I wasn't there when he awoke. I also felt guilt for stopping to pray at St. Sebastian's Catholic Church.

Glancing at my watch, I did a double take on the date. It was May 16, my ordination anniversary. I had completely forgotten about it. Then, it hit me; I no longer belonged in the sanctuary— or in this church. We were no longer Roman Catholics. On my way out, I stopped by the statue of the Blessed Virgin Mary and lit a candle, and wondered if it would be the last candle I would ever light at her feet.

Months later, on a Saturday morning, Wendy called me from her medical office. "Michael, dear lovely husband..." she said, in her sweet–talking voice.

"Yes," I said, hesitantly, knowing something was up.

"Could you bring us some coffee and muffins?"

"Sure, anything else?"

And then out of nowhere: "Yes. I think you ought to become an Episcopal Priest!"

Why not, I thought. "Okay."

"What?"

"I said, 'Okay.' "

"Really?"

The truth was, I had been thinking about the possibility of becoming an Episcopal priest for a while. When we first married, we had attended an Episcopal Church several times. I sat in the pew on my first visit and absorbed as much as I could. It was very much like a Catholic church. In fact, the inside was nicer than many Catholic churches. There was an altar and sanctuary up front, and a tabernacle with a candle burning—which meant Episcopalians believed in the Eucharist.

I opened the red Book of Common Prayer and found their catechism—a written document of the church's beliefs and teachings. Suddenly, my church history lectures from seminary took on new meaning. Thoughts of the Reformation, King Henry, Thomas More, and Anglicanism all came back and swirled around in my head. I decided to read their beliefs to find a way to justify our presence: They believed in Eucharist and Apostolic Succession; they had morning, evening and night prayers, similar to what I prayed; and they had all seven sacraments: Baptism, Eucharist, Reconciliation, Marriage, Holy Orders, Confirmation and the Anointing of the Sick.

I noted they did not believe in the "Romish Doctrine of Purgatory," devotions, adoration, or the invocation of the Saints; and, of course, the authority of the pope, which suited me. In seminary, I had agreed with a crusty old priest who had said in anger, "The Church in Rome has nothing to do with my parish!" I couldn't have said it better, so I had no misgivings about giving up the notions of purgatory and the pope.

The Anglicans and Episcopalians (same religion; one is the Church of England, while the other is the American version of the same church) hold to the doctrine of Apostolic Succession, which was important to me because it ultimately related to the Holy Eucharist. The doctrine placed the bishops and priests in direct lineage with the first Apostles, a pedigree, of sorts.

I walked into the medical office carrying Wendy's coffee and muffins. Seated in the waiting area were a man and a woman holding their newborn baby. I passed a glance their way and shared a smile. The 'I'm–a–parent–too' smile in the pediatric waiting room is the equivalent of the biker's wave; one motorcyclist lowers his left to an oncoming cyclist who usually does the same. Wendy was standing behind the glass receptionist area looking happy, which was remarkable considering she had been awake most of the night with an emergency transfer to another hospital.

"Are you serious about being an Episcopal Priest?" she asked, giving me a quick kiss.

"Yeah, why not? I mean it isn't like the pope is going to welcome married priests back or anything."

We both knew it was time to move forward.

We started attending service at All Saints Episcopal Church, a little gothic stone structure with red doors on the corner of the town square. It took a little getting used to because I didn't expect to be watching a woman priest, dressed in an alb and chasuble. Adjusting to her priestly garb was one thing, listening to her chant the preface to the Eucharistic Prayer was quite another—one that would take some getting used to.

All Saint's Episcopal became our new home. We had found a place, a church and a religion that accepted us for who we were. There was acceptance for all clergy: male and female, married and single, divorced and even openly gay. Their authority was collegial rather than papal. While there were dioceses and bishops, authority was largely exercised through conventions and bylaws, constitutions and canons. The Episcopal Church was a fit for us; perhaps I had always been a closet Episcopalian.

Wendy and I introduced ourselves to the pastor of the parish, and then arranged an appointment with Episcopal Bishop Conrad Wilson. We met for lunch at a posh country club along the shore of a private lake, where the bishop outlined his plan for us, a plan that would take about two years. First, Wendy and I would spend some time in classes to become Episcopalians. Second, I would participate in one year of individualized study with several Episcopal priests selected by the bishop, and then be eligible to be received as a priest.

"I'll use you in this diocese!" the bishop said, closing the manila folder and handing it across the table to me. "Here's what you need to do."

It seemed too good to be true: Finally, a bishop who could carry on a conversation; finally, a church where we could belong; and finally, a plan for us as a couple and a family.

At All Saint's Episcopal Church, Wendy and I became volunteers for coffee hours and nursery care. During the season of Advent, I taught a series on the Book of Revelation. Wendy would attend and laugh at me, when I would get excited about a particular Scripture passage. "You're back in your element," she would say. "You really were meant to be a priest! A married priest!"

I now had what was always missing: to be married—and a priest.

CHAPTER XXX

I paced up and down the hallway of the hospital, just a few doors from where Wendy was having her mammogram. It was her second scan since we married, and I was filled with anxiety.

Wendy's mom had died of breast cancer at the age of 44, years before Wendy and I met. Cancer had made both of us mother–orphans. Now I began projecting the dreaded illness to Wendy. What if something shows up? I asked myself.

I stopped pacing and stared out the window, looking down at the hospital parking lot. Just the other evening, Isaac and I had been sitting in the same lot, playing a game, and waiting for Wendy to finish an emergency call. Whenever Wendy was called in, we made it a family affair. Isaac and I played spaceship in the car, while she took care of the emergency. It was easy for us to spend an hour in the car, which served as our command post, our rocket ship and our star speeder, complete with a CD playing the theme from Star Wars.

I turned away from the window and walked slowly down the hallway. I thought of all the things we wanted to do as a married couple and a young family, but hadn't had time to do, like ballroom dancing, bicycling in Europe and taking Isaac to Disney World. I hadn't even finished renovating the house.

Life was passing by too quickly.

A few days later, Wendy received the unwelcome news that there were some questionable spots on the mammogram, and another scan was needed. From that moment on, and for a full week before we received new results, all we did was wait and worry. Wendy made a huge decision that week in the middle of the night. She often found solutions and made decisions as she slept, which I came to believe was simply a result of her being a genius. Her middle–of–the–night epiphany happened as I lay awake worrying and staring at the ceiling fan, spinning in a slow cadence.

Wendy sat up in bed. "Michael, are you awake?"

"Yeah."

"I reached a decision."

"Okay," I said, without moving. "What decision?"

"Even if this lump is nothing, I need to change what I am doing."

I slowly nodded. "Alright."

"If the lump is cancer, I will need to work part time during treatment so we still have an income. If it isn't, I still want to go part time. I need to be a Mom for Isaac."

I understood totally, and was actually relieved. I knew she was working too many hours, and I knew she didn't enjoy working with the physicians in her group. The cancer test had been a wake–up call.

"So that means you will need to get a job and become a part–time grad student," she said, finishing her solution.

"Fine."

Within the week, we learned the mammogram was negative. Still, we followed through with our plan. By the spring, I was employed by a private therapy group as a family therapist and Wendy's new work schedule had brought some relief.

The agency that hired me was housed in a former Catholic hospital just a short walk from our home. My office was in what used to be one of the convent bedrooms. It reminded me of my room in college seminary with the same musty old–building smell. For my first week, as part of my new employee orientation, I watched videocassette tapes and learned how to become a 'strength–based counselor.' When I wasn't watching the tapes, I wandered the abandoned hallways of the hospital. On one such break I peeked into an empty room and saw an old iron hospital bed, a metal chair and a dusty outline on the wall where a crucifix had once hung. The bed and chair looked like an eerie throwback to a horror film, but the mission crucifix struck a note of longing in my soul, like a bell tolling.

Eventually, I came across a door that said 'chapel' and opened it. Immediately my eyes darted all around looking for the tabernacle, but there was no sanctuary candle lit anywhere, no Eucharistic presence of Jesus. Chances were the chapel was no longer used for Mass, but I needed a fix—like some addict. I took a seat and blankly stared at the wooden altar in front of me.

The air conditioner kicked on, and I soaked in the coolness. I felt comforted to know Isaac was at home with my Dad, just a block away, and Wendy was now working part time at the pediatric practice, just a few minutes away.

Our plan seemed to be in place and working well; everything seemed together. I looked down at my new shirt and the laminated identification tag, and broke a smile. My job was to travel to my court–appointed clients' homes to conduct therapy, and my employer had recommended I leave my dress clothes at home, as some of the places I would be visiting were rough, hygienically speaking. Wendy had bought me some new clothes: inexpensive shirts, jeans and boots were to be my uniform.

I gazed at the empty altar and my conversation began. "Well, here I am."

It was May, near Mother's Day and my ordination anniversary. Here I was again in a Roman Church; or, in this case, what used to be a Roman Chapel.

"Thanks for Wendy and Isaac—I'd be so lost without them. Thanks for healing Wendy. Please be with Isaac and my Dad." My prayers and petitions just kept pouring out. "Help us, be with us."

I glanced at the wall to my left and noticed a niche in the wall where the statue of Mary would have been. My thoughts changed to the upcoming weekend and Mother's Day, when Wendy and I would officially become Episcopalians. I was thrilled to think that within the year as a married man, I would again be able to celebrate Holy Eucharist as an Episcopalian Priest. God was providing for us. He had given us a way to live our faith, a gift we needed to accept.

A few days later, I found myself, for the third time in my life, kneeling in front of a bishop; this time, he was an Episcopalian bishop.

Wendy and I left our pew and walked forward, stepping up into the sanctuary of the small church. People from surrounding parishes had come to extend their hands in prayer. Bishop Wilson laid his hands on us, first Wendy, and then me. "Michael, we recognize you as a member of the one holy catholic and apostolic church, and we receive you into the fellowship of this Communion. God, the Father, Son, and Holy Spirit, bless, preserve, and keep you."

Today was Mother's Day. On this very day, three years ago, I celebrated Holy Mass, gave a Mother's Day Blessing, and then took a bike ride and met the love of my life. Two years ago, I was in the hospital with Wendy and our two–day–old son, Michael Isaac. Today, again on Mother's Day, we were becoming members of a new church.

We recited the Nicene Creed, the profession of the faith, which I had done so many times. It was a prayer shared by both the Anglican/Episcopal and the Roman Church. Yet there was something deeper happening as well. I knew that by kneeling in front of this Episcopal bishop and recognizing his spiritual and pastoral authority, I was officially severing my ties to the Roman Catholic Church. I was submitting to his authority and his church, no longer connected to Rome. Rome didn't want me—didn't want us.

I knelt down as a suspended Roman Catholic priest. When I stood, I was officially an *excommunicated* Roman Catholic priest.

The people in the small church responded to the bishop's prayer with a simple "Amen."

CHAPTER XXXI

Beep, beep, beep!

The annoying electronic tone woke us from a deep midwinter snooze. "Is that yours or mine?" I asked. Wendy was already reaching for her pager and a notepad that lay on the floor by the bed.

Our lives were scheduled by other people's lives—their problems, worries, fears, anxieties, real and imagined phobias, neuroses and medical issues. It was nothing for a parent to call at nine o'clock at night, suddenly concerned, and ask Wendy what to do because the baby hadn't pooped for two days. Worse yet were a few calls about a child having an asthma attack. The child would go to the emergency room for a breathing treatment and the mom would wait in the parking lot, smoking a cigarette while talking on her cell phone. Thank God, these were rare. There were also times when Wendy served as the pediatrician for my clients.

When we first got together, I knew God would somehow take care of us. Even though the last couple of years had been rough, we were settling in and I knew it was all because of God's grace. Best of all, we were finally part of a church.

Even more remarkable was Wendy's new job. When we were attending our Episcopalian classes, a physician in a medical group in town told Wendy she was moving and suggested Wendy talk to her partner about joining the practice. Wendy had been looking for a new position with greater flexibility and control over her hours and this promised to be a perfect fit. Within weeks, Wendy had a new office to practice pediatrics and a schedule that allowed her more time to be a mom.

Everything seemed to be working out. Wendy had a normal place to work, and my job was bearable except, of course, when the pager wouldn't stop beeping.

Beep, beep, beep! "It's mine," I said.

I looked at the time flashing on the pager 1:58 a.m. I stood up and walked into our sitting room carrying the little black box that controlled my movements, emotions, and thoughts—like some type of electric dog collar. None of my clients had electric collars as far as I could tell. Some did have ankle bracelets—or what they considered as "probation jewelry". I parted the drapes and looked out the window; all of my body warmth seemed to be escaping through the soles of my feet. Great, more snow.

I prayed I didn't have to leave and go outside. A plow truck scraped its way past the house, its yellow flashing light reflecting off the houses along the road. It wasn't the snow that bothered me. It was the month–long darkness. It was dark in the morning and dark in the evening with days dragging on with about five hours of daylight and a never–ending icy mess. The combination drained my life energy.

I had put hundreds of miles on our Pontiac Grand Am, traveling throughout the county to offer hope to my court–appointed clients. The car was 10 years old, now two–tone in color: blue and rust. It was all we could afford. We had Wendy's school loans to repay and a house to renovate. However, Isaac loved the car, which he thought was a racecar with a loud booming engine. He didn't know the sound emanated from the car's broken exhaust pipe, and when I floored the gas pedal, the water pump would squeak, sounding like a bunch of rats under the hood. I often thought my clients could hear the car coming, and would know not to answer the door.

When my clients did open the door, I felt I was entering another world. Rarely did they ever talk about church, God or anything religious. I wasn't allowed to discuss or suggest either, because my position was funded by state, federal and county monies. It required developing behavior plans void of any mention of spiritual meaning or purpose. All that was left was to sell secular hope and no one really ever bought it. Sadly, it seemed that all of my clients were on antidepressants.

I dialed the phone in response to the pager, but a busy signal pulsed in my ear. "Come on, they page me and then keep using the phone."

In the bathroom, I couldn't get the hot water to kick in so I splashed some cold water on my face and over my shaved head. I looked in the mirror and wondered for a moment what happened to the famous clinical psychologist I was going to be, the one who would wear a tweed jacket and jeans and give lectures on issues that really didn't matter but were very interesting.

"Family Preservation Therapist," I said, repeating my job title aloud. "What the heck is that? I can't think of one family of mine that should be preserved. The healthy ones break up!"

I pulled on a pair of jeans and stopped my little tirade. God was good. I had a decent job and Wendy was happy. We were part of a church and soon I would be back in my element as a priest.

I reached in my closet for a sweatshirt and reminded myself that I was providing health insurance for the family. By the time I leaned over the bed and gave Wendy a kiss, I was ready to go out and save the day. As I gave her a kiss on top of her head, she snuggled tight under the blankets. "Be careful," she mumbled.

"Love you."

I walked toward the hallway, grabbed the portable phone and then went into Isaac's room and gave him a kiss and blessed him— moving my right hand and silently saying, *In the name of the Father, the Son, and the Holy Spirit.* Under the circumstances of our new life, it seemed a strange thing to do and not unlike when he was younger and I would rock him or carry him and sing in Latin the "Salve Regina," a hymn to the Blessed Virgin Mary. I was always sneaking blessings upon family members.

Beep, beep, beep! I dialed the phone again, as I walked down the stairs. "Hello?" There was yelling and screaming in the background. "Yes, this is Mr. Ripple."

"Who?" Came the reply.

"Mr. Ripple! You paged me!"

"Just a minute." They held the phone away and yelled, "Would you shut up? Shut up! Mr. Ripple?"

All I needed to know was who was on the phone so I would know where to go. "Yes. Who is this?"

"This is Fiona Ashrillow, Harold's mom... You better get over here...we found him naked doing something to the dog!"

the Priesthood: Part II

2001–2003

"The Lord has sworn and will not waiver: 'Like Melchizedek you are a priest forever.' "
—from the Book of Psalms.

CHAPTER XXXII

"I hear that you're going to be joining us here in the city," Monsignor Rosenbaum said, as he shook my hand. We were attending a wine and cheese reception celebrating the blessing of a new social hall and clergy from the nearby Roman Catholic Cathedral were invited.

The Rector of the Episcopal Cathedral, Charles Trucio stood next to us and smiled. Just a few weeks earlier, Episcopal Bishop Wilson had asked Charles to tutor me in all things Anglican and Episcopal. After a few sessions, he offered me a job on the Cathedral staff as a paid pastoral minister. We couldn't believe it. It was as though our life turned for the better as soon as we joined the Episcopal faith.

My duties at the cathedral would include hospital and home visitation, some parish education and some preaching. I was to be totally immersed in the Episcopal life and liturgy, and perform all duties except celebrate Episcopal Holy Eucharist according to the Book of Common Prayer. Then, after one year, I would assume the role of assistant priest.

The only downside was the 80–mile commute I would be making every day. However, it was a no brainer. First I had the opportunity to do ministry and actually get a decent salary for it; my salary as an Episcopal minister would be almost 50 times what I had received as a Roman Catholic priest—a perk we didn't expect. Second, there was the hope that I would one day be able to return as rector to the Episcopal church in our hometown. Thus, the job at the cathedral was a wonderful temporary two–year fit for us.

I smiled at Monsignor. "Shh," I said, as I put my finger to my lips. "Nobody knows yet. It isn't official."

Monsignor laughed. "Welcome aboard! You know you didn't stray too far from your roots. After all, Anglicans are really the first cousins to us Romans. And, man—now you've been both!"

"Yeah, wasn't there a hillbilly song called, "I Am My Own Grandpa"?"

The Monsignor made me feel comfortable for who I had become. After all, I used to be one of them; usually, I felt defensive around another Roman Catholic priest who remembered me or knew my story. He accepted me.

"And your wife, her name is?"

"Wendy." I motioned to where she stood. "She's over there, chasing our little boy, Isaac."

"Isaac," he said. "What a strong name. He must keep the two of you going...look at him!"

"He certainly does."

Both of us watched as Isaac grabbed the microphone. "You know, it sure is different preaching when your wife and son are in the pew."

"How so?" Monsignor took a sip of wine from the clear plastic cup.

"Well, just a few weeks ago, I was preaching at All Saints Episcopal, where we currently belong. It was on the Gospel of Luke, the one where the mother asks Jesus to promise her that her sons will sit at his right and left."

"Yes, we had the same Gospel. I remember."

"I ended my homily with the question, 'So, who is the greatest?' And the congregation went silent—except for a loud slurp and the sound of a binky being pulled out—then I heard, 'Me!'"

Monsignor laughed. "The little guy, huh?"

Isaac had the microphone and was getting ready to tell the only joke he knew, which, of course, involved poop. For a three-year-old, he was on top of his game as a standup comedian, and poop jokes were his specialty. Wendy looked over and gave me a great smile. I watched as she gently coaxed the microphone from Isaac. I loved the red dress she had on and the way her hair was done; I loved checking her out and watching her with my son; I loved the moment I was in—I was happy.

Just then, a woman in a wheel chair made a beeline for me. After she introduced herself as the wife of some deceased clergy, she looked up and asked, "Where is your wife?"

"She's over there with my son, Isaac." I pointed.

The woman squinted. "The one with the red dress?"

"Yes." I continued to admire my family.

"Well," she said, clearing her throat in order to speak her next opinion clearly. "She certainly doesn't look like a minister's wife!"

I took that as a compliment.

Later that summer, Wendy and I were married for the second time by Bishop Wilson in the little side chapel of the Episcopal Cathedral of St. John. Employing clergy who had been married in a civil union rather than one blessed in the Episcopal Church could raise some eyebrows, so we needed a religious ceremony to abide by the canon laws of the church.

Father Jerry, uncle to Isaac, made the long drive to be with us. Though he did not participate in the ceremony, he joined us for the reception. I didn't want it to be that way—I wanted all of us to receive from the same altar. Part of me understood and part of me did not.

At the conclusion of the liturgy, Bishop Wilson came over to Wendy and me and said, "This time it took!" The three of us laughed. He was referring to the letter I had received from the Roman Catholic bishop when I first left the priesthood. It notified me that I was officially suspended as a priest because I had "attempted marriage."

Six months after our church marriage, I became a full–fledged Episcopal priest. On the Feast of All Saints, I knelt before the bishop and promised obedience to the Rites, Sacraments, and Authority of the Episcopal and Anglican Church. I then stepped up into the mosaic–tiled sanctuary and signed a book, which lay open on the altar. It was official.

That day, I believed with all my heart that God was meeting Wendy and me where we were, urging us to move forward and offering the Episcopal Church as His gift to us. Not only did God help us find a home and a community of faith for ourselves, He had once again chosen me as a priest for His people.

The following day, after a five–year absence, I stood behind the altar and prepared to offer the consecratory prayers over the bread and wine. I looked out at the congregation and smiled at Wendy, Isaac and my Dad. I raised my folded hands and pressed my index fingers to my lips sending a secret kiss to Wendy and Isaac. Before me on the altar was my new chalice and patent given to me by family and friends. I opened the Book of Common Prayer and began the Eucharistic Prayer.

From that day forward, every time I prayed the Anglican Eucharistic Prayer I was transported to a different time and place. The words and phrasings were so similar to the ones that I used to say when I was a Roman Catholic priest that I often became confused.

Every time I took the host, I said the words of consecration: *Take, eat. This is my Body, which is given for you. Do this for the remembrance of me.* Every time I took the chalice in my hands, I prayed: *Drink this, all of you. This is my Blood of the new Covenant, which is shed for you and for many for the forgiveness of sins.*

Every time I prayed the words, I felt just a little off. I knew they would soon become second nature to me, just as the old Roman prayers had. For once, I had no agenda, no ecumenical or even ecclesial aspirations. All I wanted to do was celebrate Holy Eucharist and the other sacraments.

The other sacraments were few and far between during my two years at the cathedral. There was not a single baptism, and forget about hearing anyone's confession—it just wasn't practiced. As to the Sacrament of Anointing of the Sick, I celebrated it most often during hospital visits, usually confusing the words, which probably made most of my anointing's illicitly Roman Catholic.

In addition, I had few wedding celebrations, but in all honesty—most couples wouldn't have noticed even if I had done a Buddhist ceremony. Yet, the Episcopal Sacrament of Matrimony and the Funeral Rite were very similar to the Roman Catholic celebrations.

Preaching was stressed more in the Episcopal tradition than in my Roman schooling. I was preaching from my real experiences of love, marriage and fatherhood. Yellow Post–It notes and drawings from Isaac decorated my black Book of Common Prayer. I carried it as I preached, walking the aisle and sanctuary. My life was more connected to my preaching, and I loved it. During office time, I furthered my studies in Anglicanism, theology and spirituality. I even pursued some continued education in family systems and clinical psychology.

No one sought any spiritual counseling at the Cathedral. Instead, I was the one who dealt with the walk–ins, the people in need of food, shelter and usually some cash. I enjoyed listening to the multitude of stories that accompanied each request and occasionally used some old therapist tricks to help them along. I always invited them to come back on Sunday for church and some food. Only one ever came to the service, and gave me a big wave, as he shuffled into the pew. After the service, I invited him to stay for coffee and donuts.

During my Roman days, the friendships and community shared by clergy were central to the celibate's life. Community among fellow clergy was not as important in the Episcopal life for a variety of reasons. Geographically there was a greater distance between parishes. Many of the clergy were married or in some relationship and had familial commitments. Most notably, however, was the simple fact that Episcopal priests were autonomous from the diocese and each other. The relationship was more administrative. If necessary, an Episcopal priest could apply for a new parish or position anywhere in the world, at any time—kind of like a free–agent priest. Knowing that I could go anywhere with my family and be an Episcopal priest gave me a tremendous sense of freedom.

I finally had some peace; we finally had some peace.

CHAPTER XXXIII

The snow was blowing across the interstate making it impossible to do anything except follow the line of red car lights in front of you. I was slowly being hypnotized by the white flakes flying horizontally into the windshield. Wendy was starting to nod off, and Isaac was sound asleep in the back seat.

Beep, beep, beep! Wendy's pager broke the silence. "That's Frank's number," she said, looking at the screen. She quickly dialed her work partner's cell phone. "Hello, Frank?"

He started right into it, "I'm sorry kiddo, but I don't know if you still have a job."

Despite the high drama of the moment, the story came to a quick ending. Frank retired and with little choice in the matter, we became the proud parents of a new pediatric medical practice, one born entirely out of necessity. Just like the first few months of parenthood, it was one of the most chaotic times of our lives.

Wendy quickly became reacquainted with her old friend, long hours. Her days consisted of two early morning hours of making hospital rounds, eight hours of office visits and every evening on call; she rounded out the week with weekend call and bookkeeping. What had happened to her dream of working as a part–time physician?

I learned the meaning of the word multitask: priest by day; and by evening, medical office support staff, maintenance man, computer specialist and errand boy. In between, I was spending nearly two hours commuting from job to job.

During this time, I began having a recurring dream: A hideous creature—one I knew was demonic—would hover over me and push down on me as I lay in bed. I knew I needed to protect Isaac and Wendy, but I could not move. Suddenly, I would utter a deep, throaty moan of terror and jump out of the bed, pushing the creature away.

Wendy and I would laugh it off in the morning as a bad dream generated by stress and fatigue. However, I privately worried about the dream's meaning. I was not so sure it was a dream.

One morning at my day job as an Episcopalian priest, I sat alone on an ornately carved wooden seat, tucked into the side of the cathedral sanctuary. On the shelf in the kneeler were my prayer books. This was my space. It was where I would sit anytime there was a liturgy or service. I looked to my left and saw the red candle burning next to the tabernacle or, as Episcopalians called it, the ambry.

I reached forward, grabbed my Episcopal prayer book, and moved the ribbon to the current day, closed the book and closed my eyes. I wondered when I would begin to feel that I was moving closer to God. I had hoped becoming an Episcopal priest would bring me closer in my relationship with Jesus Christ. Instead, I felt like a man with a good–paying job. I started to wonder on that day what had gone wrong.

All the while life seemed to be spinning crazy fast. On one recent Sunday, when I had come home from service, Isaac would not wait for me to change. He, Wendy and my brother led me across the street, up the ally and into the parking lot of a funeral home where his bike was leaning against a tree. He hopped on and started pedaling without training wheels and yelled, "Happy Father's Day, Dad!"

I leaned my head against the cathedral seat, and smiled at my memory of Isaac's bike ride. I loved watching Wendy laugh, smile and applaud her little boy. I thought about the time I wrecked on my bike when I was seven and how my mother held me in the back of the ambulance.

I closed my eyes and soaked in the stillness of God—not consciously trying to do anything. I took a few deep breaths and on my exhale, said the word, "love." Slowly I went deeper and deeper: love, I thought of Wendy; love, I thought of Isaac; love, I thought of God.

The next morning I went back to my cathedral seat. I liked the feeling I had the day before of sitting with Jesus, something I always preached but had failed to follow. I pulled a set of Anglican prayer beads out of my pocket. Wendy had told me about them a few months back, and I ordered three pair on the internet. Holding the blue shiny beads in my hand, I decided it was really just an abbreviated rosary; as I examined the cross I saw there was no cor-pus, no little metal Jesus hanging on the cross; just a plain cross.

I was not sure I liked the idea of Anglican prayer beads. Thus, I prayed the only prayer that comes to my heart every time fingers touch a bead, almost as a spiritual reflex: *Hail Mary, full of grace…*

CHAPTER XXXIV

I sat opposite Bishop Wilson's desk. "They can't afford to pay you," he said, in response to my question.

I had come to the bishop to ask if there was a place for me at All Saint's Episcopal, near our home. The distance to the cathedral made my work commute difficult and kept our family from becoming part of the congregation. All Saint's Episcopal needed a physical and spiritual renewal and I wanted the challenge. It was where we lived and with Wendy owning the medical practice, had put down roots. Unlike years ago, I seemed to have found my niche and enjoyed being a parish priest so much that now I believed I was ready to be a pastor.

The bishop cleared his throat and leaned forward. "Look, All Saint's has no money, they can't afford you."

"I am willing to take a pay cut."

He continued, "This isn't public yet, but Saint Paul's, just south of the city and closer to you, is going to need an interim minister. Ed Wingard is retiring. You go and get certified as an interim minister and then you take St. Paul's for a year or two; then after that, see if anything else opens up." With that said, Bishop Wilson sat back in his chair—problem solved.

Three months later, I unlocked the door and walked into my new office at St. Paul Episcopal Church. The furniture was magnificent, comparable to décor found in a corporate CEO's office. There was a burgundy couch, two upholstered chairs, a coffee table, three huge bookcases, and a vast mahogany desk with built-in file drawers. Years ago, I would have been scandalized with such a set up. Now I had come to expect it.

I walked over to the window and lifted a slat on the wooden window blind. Just outside my office was a manicured courtyard with the look of a Virginian estate. The morning sun cast its light through the crystal clear windows of the redbrick church to my left. There was no stained glass in this part of the Episcopal world; St. Paul's was considered a low church—the exact opposite of the cathedral.

The bishop had asked me to do several things during my two-year assignment. Most importantly, he wanted me to bring the congregation back to celebrating the Holy Eucharist every Sunday. They had been in the practice of alternating Holy Eucharist with Morning Prayer; they would do Morning Prayer, then break for coffee and donuts, and then go back in the church for Holy Communion, almost as an afterthought. His final requests: Find out what was going on with the parish school, conduct an audit and start the search for a new rector.

I took my first phone call in my new office. "Hello, this is Father Ripple."

"I can't believe what they did!" The man's voice was rough and angry.

"Sir, I'm sorry, but I don't know what you are talking about. May I ask your name?"

"That don't matter—I just want you to know that I think the Episcopal Church is going to Hell."

"Why?"

"Because they made that fag a bishop! There is no morality in the Episcopal Church."

At least, now I understood the issue. One week prior, the American Episcopal Church affirmed the election of an openly gay bishop, with a male living partner. It had upset the entire Anglican and Episcopal Church and set the course for a schism. To some, the choice of a gay bishop was a step toward gay marriage liturgy and a long slippery slope of moral, ethical and theological dilemmas. With that decision, the Episcopal Church accepted moral relativism as fundamental to its nature, a stance I could not support. Maybe I used up all my liberal juice when I left the Roman Catholic Church, but I felt the leadership of the Episcopal Church was spiritually out of sync.

"Sir, I can't speak for their reasoning. My only concern at this moment is St. Paul's—I just started as the interim rector today. You are my first phone call." I hoped to make the mood a little lighter.

"Well, I just think it's a sin, and the Episcopal Church is going to Hell."

"Sir, would you like to come in and talk about this?"

"No. I'm not Episcopalian."

"Well then, what are you?"

"I'm Roman Catholic."

"What?"

"I'm Roman Catholic."

"So…why…are you calling…me?"

Where did he get off fighting this battle when his own church had sex scandals filling the headlines? For the past year Roman Catholic sex scandals, priest pedophilia, cover–ups and payoffs were providing weekly stories for the media. I told him that his church had issues of its own, and he should help with that clean up and stay out of our house.

"Goodbye," I said, and slammed the phone, then thought, self–righteous Catholics!

Just then, Elizabeth, the parish secretary walked into my office. "Wow, you sure told him!"

"I'm sorry. He just got under my skin."

She busied herself straightening the window blind that I had made crooked. "You know, Father Michael…I'm…I'm Roman Catholic."

I pushed my chair back from the desk and quickly stood up. "Oh no!"

"What?" She stepped back. "What's wrong? What did I do?"

"You're a Roman Catholic?"

"Yes."

"Well then, you can no longer work here."

I walked to the door, turned the knob, and looked back at Elizabeth. All the color had drained from her face. "I'm joking, Elizabeth."

I slowly walked down the hallway and into the church. I genuflected and sat on a red velvety cushioned pew and looked around. There was a shiny gold collection plate propped up on the credence table to the left of the altar, staring right back at me. To the right of it was a thin metal cross, about four feet long, which hung in front of plush dark burgundy drapes. I kept looking around for a crucifix, but couldn't find one anywhere in the sanctuary or in the church. I did notice the red sanctuary candle sticking out from the wall burning next to the tabernacle.

I got up, meandered down the center aisle and up the burgundy-carpeted steps, and stood behind the altar. I raised my arms, as if I were saying, "Let us pray!" I moved over to the lectern and stood where the Holy Scriptures are proclaimed.

"When I was in seminary," I said, projecting in a deep voice, "someone put forth the proposition that you could petition the Lord with prayer...."

I was committing a preaching sacrilege, first by grabbing the sides of the lectern (driving the podium), and second by quoting rock star Jim Morrison. I looked over my right shoulder and saw the tabernacle, which was built into the wall. Walking over, I noticed the red sanctuary candle wasn't a candle, but an electric bulb. I genuflected and opened the door.

I couldn't believe what I saw.

I never thought of myself as super–critical or particular, but this caused me pain. I reached in and gently pulled out a plastic Ziploc sandwich bag. I raised it to my eyes and counted ten small Hosts. God didn't warrant any ciborium or special dish or even a plastic Rubbermaid container. No, the Body of Christ was in a plastic baggie.

What a morning it had been.

Cancer *and* Healing

2003

*"Daughter, your faith has saved you. Go in peace
and be cured of your affliction."*
—from the Gospel of Jesus Christ according to Mark.

CHAPTER XXXV

"That was a great bicycle ride," I said, while reaching to turn on the shower.

"Yeah, but it made me hungry. I'm starving."

Wendy turned and directed her voice out the bathroom and down the steps. "Isaac, you're next when you're Dad and I are finished taking our shower."

"Isaac?" She raised her voice another notch.

"Yeah," he hollered back. He and my brother, Uncle George, were downstairs wrestling on the kitchen floor.

Wendy slipped off her black bike shorts and shirt. Her face was still red from the ride, and her thick loopy curls were pushed down and flattened by the bike helmet. Her skin was tanned, toned, and shiny from her sweat and her legs were firm and defined. She caught me checking her out and smiled. She stepped past me into the shower, reaching to adjust the water just a little more.

It was a great bathroom. We had just finished it a few weeks ago. From beige ceramic tile with raised Mediterranean designs to new oak wainscoting, indirect lighting, an antique sink table and etched shower glass—the bathroom was planned and perfect.

The sun was setting and casting its glow on two reliefs we'd bought at Niagara–on–the–Lake, during one of our wine–tasting excursions, when Isaac thought he was drunk from drinking his fizzy grape juice and kept saying that he "felt a little woozy." Out the window, I could see our newly finished deck. Six light–up stars dangled from the wood beams above the hot tub—transforming it into our imaginary mountain hot spring. Isaac's wooden play set was carefully situated amidst the mulch and behind a white privacy fence, which protected our sacred space.

Not too long ago the deck had been filled with people celebrating Pappy's 80th birthday. Everyone had huddled for a group picture. Wendy was nestled next to me, with a gentle hand on Isaac, trying to keep him from making bunny ears behind Pappy. Being in family pictures has always filled me with anxiety. I remembered the last picture I had taken of my mother.

I looked back at Wendy in the shower and noticed she was feeling her left breast.

"Feel this." She took my right hand, and pushing down, led my fingers across her soft breast to a lump.

Our eyes met. We knew. The water cascaded over our bodies and disappeared down the drain—that planned, perfect drain.

CHAPTER XXXVI

I reached forward and pushed the On Star button on the dashboard of my new Saab turbo wagon, a birthday gift from Wendy. "Hello, welcome to OnStar."

"Get mail," I said, into the speaker.

In an instant, my emails were being read to me. I glanced at the time on the clock and calculated when I would be finished at the Diocesan House and when I would eventually arrive at St. Paul's. Then I called my office. "Elizabeth, I have to drop off these registration forms for the Diocesan Convention. I'll probably be a little late. I'm supposed to meet with someone this morning—I can't remember who, just tell them to sit tight."

"Fine, Father Michael."

"Elizabeth?"

"Yes, Father?"

"Could you please just call me Michael?"

"Okay Faa—I mean Michael."

The truth was I couldn't remember my meeting because I wasn't able to focus on anything, not parishioners, not the Diocesan Convention and not Episcopal Church business—only Wendy.

I ended the phone call, and continued to think and worry about Wendy. A couple of days had passed since Wendy had a biopsy, and we had received some assurance that it was probably nothing more than fibrous tissue. We hoped it would end as just another close call.

I parked in the lot next to the Episcopal Cathedral and made my way into the Diocesan House. After chatting with the bishop's secretary, I gave her the paperwork and walked towards the back entrance, stopping in the restroom. I heard the office telephone ring when I was washing my hands. When I stepped into the hallway, the secretary spotted me and hollered, "Michael, you have a phone call on line one."

I walked into the copy room, picked up the receiver, and pushed the flashing red button. "Hello?"

"Michael!"

"Wendy?"

"Michael!" Her voice began rising to a cry.

"Oh God, no!"

The next thing I knew, I was sitting behind Wendy's desk at her medical office, waiting for her to come in. I could still smell the new paint. We had just finished remodeling the place two weeks ago. Everything was brand new: chairs, file cabinets, furniture, refrigerators, employee lockers, water cooler and even artwork.

Uncle George, stood staring out the window, sniffling and holding back tears. I noticed a mild tremor in his right hand.

The door opened, and Wendy walked in. She had just been diagnosed with cancer and now she had only 60 seconds to hold onto her husband. Wendy had to keep seeing and healing her young patients; she had to keep smiling to keep them from being afraid.

That night Wendy, Isaac and I lay on the air mattress in our bedroom. We had bought new bedroom furniture but it had not yet been delivered. I had to pump more air into the mattress because it had a slow leak, which would have been fun and cool any other night—but not tonight. Isaac was nestled against his mother and soon fell asleep. The sight split my heart. I sat on the floor next to her. With my fingers, I traced designs in the plush carpet, remembering when we had chosen it at the store. Tonight, everything was a memory.

I watched as she caressed Isaac's hair.

"What do you need?"

It was an odd question, but it just came out. Perhaps I was hoping that if I just knew what she needed then I could find it, bring it back, and the cancer would be gone.

"I need Father Freed. I need the Holy Spirit."

Wendy turned her head away and held onto Isaac. Her body shook as she stifled her crying, careful not to wake Isaac. I got up, walked into the sitting room and dialed Uncle Jerry. He knew we were waiting for the biopsy results. "Wendy has breast cancer."

"I'm sorry, Michael."

"Hey Jerry, I need Eph's phone number—do you have a directory near you?"

"Sure, just a minute."

I immediately dialed Eph's rectory and left a message, "Eph, it's Rip. Please give me a call whenever you get this message. I don't care what time it is, I need you to call me. It's about Wendy. Thanks."

Back in the room, I sat on the floor next to the mattress. Waves of shock and sorrow washed over me. No one I knew had ever survived cancer. I looked at Isaac sound asleep and cried out silently to God: Give it to me! Take me! I held Wendy's hands. That was all we could do—sit and hold hands.

I closed my eyes and whispered, "God, just give us some hope, some sign that we'll be Okay." I knew I shouldn't be praying for a sign, but I just wanted His will to be mine.

The phone rang. I looked at the caller ID. "It's Eph."

Within 24 hours, Wendy, Isaac, Pappy, Uncle George and I were sitting in the parking lot of Eat'n Park, off the interstate exit, waiting for Ephraim. We had eaten here about a month ago, when we came to the outlets to buy school clothes for Isaac to start kindergarten. I kept glancing in the rearview mirror at Isaac. Uncle George and he were having fun counting and naming the different cars.

"There he is."

I pointed at Eph's car pulling into a parking space.

Wendy watched him as he got out of his car. "I thought he was much taller. I remember him being bigger. Are you sure that's him, Michael?"

"Well, that man is dressed like a priest," I said, helplessly offering some humor.

Following dinner, we drove to a small Catholic church where Eph was celebrating a healing Mass. I rode with him while Uncle George drove Wendy, Isaac and Pappy. I was trying to put it all together but I didn't know what "it" was that I needed to put together.

The shadows from the trees flashed across the road and appeared to dance on the road. "Some people get seizures from that," I said, explaining what Wendy had told me years ago, as we drove on mountain roads with the same moving images. I looked back at my family in the car behind us. "I hope the cancer didn't spread."

"Me too," Ephraim said.

At the church, Eph went back into the sacristy and we sat in the front pew. I knelt down and looked at the tabernacle. It had been a few years since I'd been in a Catholic Church. Isaac started getting bored so the two of us took a walk. As we came back into the church, Isaac whispered, "Dad?"

"Yeah buddy?"

"What are those voices?"

"Oh, those are the people praying the rosary." My son had never heard a rosary being said before Mass.

"Why are they praying out loud?"

"Well, that's just something that they do."

"Why don't we do that at your church?"

For a moment, I felt Roman Catholic; maybe the Holy Spirit didn't get the word I had been excommunicated.

After Communion, Father Ephraim began the prayers for healing and people began filing into the sanctuary. I watched Wendy as she stood next to me with her eyes closed. As Ephraim blessed her, she fell backwards into the arms of a large man, waiting to catch anyone who rested in the Holy Spirit. He caught her and let her gently rest on the floor. I watched and prayed so hard for healing to come into her body. I imagined the tumor dissolving and disappearing.

Next, Ephraim came to Isaac. As he gently placed his hand on Isaac's head, Isaac began to teeter and sway. Eph reached out and held Isaac close to him. His priestly garment, the chasuble, enveloped and covered Isaac, as he tenderly rested in Ephraim's arms. My eyes welled up.

Then Eph laid his right hand on my head. I closed my eyes and fell.

When I came to, I heard sobbing—loud hyperventilating sobbing. I looked up, saw the ceiling of the church and tried to move, but for a moment I was glued to the floor. I recognized the crying; it was my four–year–old son, Isaac.

By the time I got up, Wendy was carrying Isaac down the center aisle and out the doors. The three of us sat outside on a stone banister. You could still hear the organ music playing in the Church. George and Pappy eventually made their way outside to us. Isaac's big brown eyes were full of tears, and he was trying to catch his breath between sobs. Wendy held him and I held Wendy. It was very dark; there were no stars, no moon and no light.

"Shh, everything's alright," Wendy said, rocking him and lovingly stroking his hair.

"What's wrong, little buddy? Why you crying? You afraid?" I thought the whole experience might have scared him.

"No," he said, sniffling.

"What is it then?" we asked, in unison.

He looked up at us and said in a little voice, "I felt God—I felt God go in me."

The words rang through the dark night—that night of healing.

CHAPTER XXXVII

"Wendy! Wendy!"

I kept yelling her name, as she lay limp in my arms on the bathroom floor, her legs and arms contorted. She had just vomited and passed out. Pappy was in his room—he didn't hear any of what was going on. Isaac was sound asleep in his room. Just two hours ago, everything was fine. Now, less than 24 hours into her first dose of chemotherapy, she was passed out in my arms. "God. Wendy! Come on, wake up!"

I kept moving her head from side to side and pleading with her. Her eyelids were open halfway and her eyes rolled back. I held her close to me and rocked back and forth on the floor, praying she'd wake up.

She came to, just long enough for me to get her into the car and over to the emergency room, just a few blocks away. At the hospital she passed out again. I watched the monitor on the wall, showing nothing but a straight green line. A loud electronic tone sounded.

"God, no! Wendy!" I cried. The doctors and nurses pushed me out of the room and drew the curtain shut. All I heard was the flat tone of the monitor. Time stopped. I thought of Isaac asleep at home, and how just a few hours before his Mom had given him a kiss good night.

A nurse ran out and I pulled the drapes back to see Wendy lying motionless on the gurney. A doctor and nurse watched the monitor as another nurse pushed past me with a cart. Just then Wendy's eyes opened and she stared at the doctor. "I'm scared."

"So am I," he said.

CHAPTER XXXVIII

A December wind howled rattling the windows in the meeting hall. The sun had already set and the shortest, darkest day of the year was fast approaching. The liturgical season of Advent was upon us. Christians throughout the world, as they have done for centuries, were counting down to Christmas—the Feast of the Incarnation of God made Man—the birth of Jesus Christ.

I stood before more than 60 parishioners of St. Paul's Episcopal Church, seated around the old heavy plywood meeting tables. After a month into the interim ministry, some people from St. Paul's had decided I was to become their next rector. It was a good offer. "Thank you," I said, and motioned for them to stop applauding.

Bishop Wilson had just endorsed me for the job of rector, following the former rector's retirement, but had warned the parishioners that I would bring change and growth to St. Paul's. The gathering had nodded in agreement and applauded. I felt my cheeks grow warm and knew that I was blushing. I cleared my throat just as another gust of winter wind rattled the rafters and whistled through the windows. Everyone looked up at the ceiling, startled by the loud sound.

"Thank you for your affirmation. I'd like to announce the fund drive for a new church roof." I began as the wind continued to howl. I waited for the laughter to die down.

"This certainly isn't the way I ever intended to accept the position of being a rector—let alone the rector at St. Paul's. I am sorry that my family can't be here," I said. "Wendy is still recovering from last week's chemo treatment. Thanks again for all your prayers."

I wished then for Wendy to be standing beside me to share in this moment, but I had much to be thankful for, especially Wendy's recovery and healing. Following that night in the emergency room, a stay in cardiac care, and a visit to a cardiologist back home, Wendy and her physicians determined that her course of chemotherapy treatment needed to be changed. This also meant she could not maintain her working schedule as planned. Suddenly, in addition to the stress of cancer and chemotherapy, both of us now faced eventual unemployment. Life was once again moving us.

As the months unfolded, it felt like we had an infusion of grace. We hunkered down through the winter and 200–mile roundtrips for chemotherapy. We closed the medical practice and I continued to make the long drives to the parish. Isaac seized the moment relishing his time with his stay–at–home Mommy. Patience, hope, fortitude, wisdom, and peace seemed to stay with us as we lived day by day. Still, a serenity rested upon us.

My prayers changed somewhat; I became more silent. At St. Paul's I'd sit in the sanctuary with the presence of Christ in His sacred Body, the Host. At night, prayer was for Wendy and Isaac asking for intercession from my mother and Wendy's mother—both dead from cancer. I also felt the quiet presence of another mother—the Mother of God.

Then, out of the blue, the position as full time rector at St. Paul's was offered to me. A few days later, Wendy was offered a new position as a pediatrician after her treatments and our move. We knew we couldn't have orchestrated these things; our prayers were being answered.

Before I arrived that night for the special meeting at St. Paul's, I had spent most of the day unpacking and setting up our Christmas decorations for what would be the last Christmas in our old house before we moved. Wendy sat on the couch making homemade ornaments out of pipe cleaners with Isaac as I set up our ceramic Christmas village and train all the while hoping and praying we would have many more years of Christmas memories to unpack.

Wendy loved Christmas, and I loved that about her. On our first Christmas together, I was putting up my train display in the empty dining room when Wendy walked in and said, "Where's the caboose Michael, your train needs a caboose!"

I took Wendy's picture of her sitting on the floor with our three dogs opening presents on Christmas morning. She was pregnant with Isaac and her cheeks were all red and flushed. One of my presents was a red caboose. Just as our life had fallen apart months ago with Wendy's diagnosis, our life was slowly starting to reassemble.

It truly was Christmas.

the Rector's World

2003–2005

"And Jesus wept."
—from the Gospel of Jesus Christ according to John.

CHAPTER XXXIX

Life was ideal.

We joined the local country club where Wendy, Isaac, Pappy and I would grab an occasional dinner. Sometimes after my last service on Sunday, we would stop by for brunch. On the way to our seats, I usually had to work the room—making sure I waved to all of the parishioners who were there. Once or twice a month I'd meet with a few of the more influential power brokers of the congregation. At those meetings I'd try to garner support for a new vision for St. Paul's.

As a first step, I began celebrating Eucharist at both services on every Sunday. There was some initial objection, but I used the bishop's mandate to move the process forward. I also found support in the results of a parish–wide survey, which showed that a majority wanted weekly Eucharist at both services. These steps toward a Eucharistic–centered worship would help to move the community back to the roots of the faith.

I saw other ways to move toward my vision, such as adding chapel time for the preschool children and inviting their families to join the parish. I hoped to add a wing to the existing church complex and offer overnight spirituality workshops and institutes. I also wanted to begin hosting weekend ecumenical retreats.

My friend Father Ephraim, with the permission of his Roman Catholic bishop, made the trip north for two healing services at St. Paul's. I celebrated Holy Eucharist and following the service, Eph led the people in prayers for healing. Together, we distributed the blessings. About 20 people were at the first service but attendance grew to more than 80 in just three months.

Following the first healing service, Eph shared with us over dinner that his gift of healing was given to him while he was on pilgrimage in Medjugorje. My eyes met Wendy's across the dinner table. We both felt something at the exact same time, a stirring in our hearts.

Wendy commented a few days later that we ought to look into that "Medjugorje thing", as she put it. She took it upon herself to gather books on the subject, while I was busy with a growing parish.

On Sundays, the pews were filling and I sensed a buzz of excitement in the parish. Of course, not everyone welcomes change, and there were a select few who didn't want to go where I was leading. As time went on, they won over others in the congregation and their numbers grew. As much as I tried not to succumb to the negativity, I had to deal with complaints on a weekly basis.

Hurtful gossip also made its way back to me: Wendy and I were not open and hospitable enough about inviting parishioners to our home, or we invited the wrong ones; Wendy didn't attend the correct Sunday service; she was the rector's wife and needed to host a Sunday coffee and doughnuts, despite her duties as a pediatrician. When Wendy talked with parents of a child who was bullying Isaac, they did not try to find a solution, but instead left the parish and blamed us.

Before long, I was defending every decision to my challengers—from wanting to form new lay committees, to celebrating Stations of the Cross during Lent, to where I put the snow shovel.

One day, I removed a chair from where it sat—unused and without purpose—near the altar in the sanctuary. With that simple act, I had committed a sin tantamount to sacrilege, albeit furniture sacrilege, because someone had donated the chair.

I also heard complaints from some volunteers who didn't want me nosing around in their kingdoms. I quickly learned that what some of the people really wanted was a lay–run approach with a puppet minister rather than a priest. Jesus sealed in a Ziploc baggie was indicative of a much deeper spiritual malaise.

Every two weeks I would have to ask for my paycheck; every month, I would ask the vestry, the lay–elected leadership of the parish, to give the okay for an outside audit. The paycheck was chronically late and the approval for an audit never came.

Whenever the phone rang at the parish office I felt anxious and worried that yet another complaint about something I did or didn't do was coming. I kept my promise of initiating new internal and external evangelization efforts. I attempted to change the format of the parish newsletter; of course, it was not well received.

Halfway through my first year, I began taking anti–anxiety medication because I was worrying about everything—especially Wendy's health. If she had a headache, a bone ache or any type of pain, to me it was cancer. She often tried to reassure me that she had been healed.

I began going door–to–door in a nearby neighborhood, inviting each household to come try out St. Paul's. Months back I had asked members on the vestry to walk with me, but no one had accepted the invitation despite their repeated comments that we needed to reach out so the church would grow. Only one older man in the congregation, who had supported my efforts from day one, would walk with me. We looked like two Mormons on a summer mission, working the streets and inviting everyone we met to visit the church and enter a deeper relationship with Christ.

One day after another recruiting walk, again alone, I returned to the office. Elizabeth was sitting behind her desk. "How'd it go?"

"Oh, I don't know. There were a few who showed interest." I picked up a stack of mail and started sorting it.

"You're doing a good thing, Father Michael, and you're doing what you said you were going to do!"

"Yeah," I said, in a halfhearted response.

"Don't worry. Look at how full Sunday's have been! People like you and what you have planned."

"Thanks for noticing, Elizabeth. Of course, you haven't switched yet!"

"No—my mother would shoot me! I don't think I could become Episcopalian—especially here. I just wish the Pope would let priests marry. You'd be great at my church!"

"There's no way priests will ever be allowed to marry," I answered with a noted tone of bitterness. I walked into my office and emerged with my prayer book in hand and added, "It would cost the Church way too much in finding rectories that separated the married with families and the single ones. I added with a rueful note, "Then, what if the gays start marrying? Think of the bachelor parties!"

Elizabeth slowly shook her head and with a caustic smile said, "You're bad!"

"Yeah, you're right. I better go pray," I said, leaving the office and walking down the hallway into the church. I sat down in a pew and glanced at the sanctuary thinking it would look so much better with long windows and a wooden crucifix instead of the red drape and thin metal cross.

After a while I opened my old Roman Catholic breviary. The ribbons were worn and the pages were yellow, but they were full of memories. On some pages I had scribbled a note or a prayer or a date I wanted to remember. There were some homemade prayers I had written, ranging from apostolic zeal to desire for union and pleading for forgiveness. My sister Claudia had given the book to me when I was ordained a deacon; in it her family had written notes of congratulation. On the back inside cover was a drawing by Isaac, and stuck to another page was a sticker reminding me what weight fly–fishing line was on my spool.

I slid the ribbon open to the page and whispered the psalm:

In you, O Lord, I take refuge.
Let me never be put to shame.
In your justice, set me free,
Hear me and speedily rescue me.

Be a rock of refuge for me,
A mighty stronghold to save me,
For you are my rock, my stronghold.
For your name's sake, lead me and guide me.

Release me from the snares they have hidden
For you are my refuge, Lord.
Into your hands I commend my spirit.
It is you who will redeem me, Lord.

O God of truth, you detest
Those who worship false and empty gods.
As for me, I trust in the Lord:
Let me be glad and rejoice in your love.

You have seen my affliction
And taken heed of my soul's distress,
Have not handed me over to the enemy,
But set my feet at large.
Bow down and hear me, Lord: come to my rescue.

Glory be to the Father, Son, and Holy Spirit
As it was in the beginning, so now and evermore, Amen.

I shut the book, closed my eyes and prayed, "God, be with this parish. Be with those who like me and those who hate me. Help them to see that I am trying to lead them on the right path. God, please, break into the life of this parish—break into me."

That evening Wendy showed me one of the books she had been reading about the apparitions of the Blessed Virgin at Medjugorje. It made me nervous. I had first seen the book as a deacon 15 years ago when someone left a copy of it outside my rectory bedroom door. It was one of the type of books I assumed were usually read by Catholic Mary–fanatic–arch–conservative–blue–haired types; that was my opinion at the time and I quickly tossed it into the garbage can.

The book was titled, *Medjugorje: The Message*, written by a man named Wayne Weible, who was a Lutheran Protestant. That was indeed strange—a Protestant writing about apparitions of the Blessed Virgin Mary. Since I was technically a "Protestant minister" now, the story held a different connection for me.

According to the book, the Blessed Virgin was allegedly appearing in a little village by that name, which was located somewhere in Yugoslavia; the author had a major spiritual conversion because of it.

I forced a "that's nice" response to Wendy as she handed me the book.

"I know you think it's wacko—but you should read it!" She smiled and left the room.

Maybe she's right, I thought, maybe I will...

CHAPTER XL

Vacation couldn't arrive fast enough. We rented a U–Haul trailer, loaded it with our bicycles, hooked it onto the back of the Toyota Highlander and headed to Gettysburg, Pennsylvania for the week. It felt good to go back home. We concluded our vacation with a visit to the shrine at Emmitsburg, Maryland.

I slowly drove up the mountain road leading to the shrine and commented, "Man, would you look at all these cars? What's going on?"

Isaac pressed his face against the glass. "There are cars everywhere, Dad!"

"Yes, there are," I responded to Isaac as I pulled the Toyota and trailer parallel onto a grassy spot. Wendy opened her door and checked to see if I was far enough off the road. Pappy and Isaac hopped out of the backseat and Wendy stood by her open door to put a leash on our new puppy, Jackson. "Michael, I need to get some water out of the back for him."

After Jackson drank some water, the five of us sauntered aimlessly past the familiar giant three–story gold statue of the Virgin

Mary. This was sacred ground where I felt the peace. Bells began their noontime toll as I walked behind Wendy, Isaac and my Dad.

I watched as Isaac pleaded with his mother to hold Jackson's leash. It was great watching the two of them from afar, especially observing Wendy being his mom. I loved that my Dad was walking with them, wondering what was going on in his head; maybe he was thinking that the last time he was here was over 25 years ago, and Mom had been walking beside him. I wondered what my Dad's prayers were like.

It seemed that all creation chimed in—locusts, cicadas and crickets—with the tolling of the bells. As the last toll reverberated across the valley, I heard the shriek of a hawk.

"Jackson!" Isaac hollered. He and Wendy were entangled in the leash, now wrapped around the two of them. I caught up and helped untangle them. Isaac spun around in circles to get undone. "Woo...I'm dizzy."

In the distance, I heard a barely audible drone of voices coming from somewhere in the woods just ahead of us: *Hail Mary, full of grace...*

My pulse beat at a nervous uncomfortable rate as suddenly, my old Roman blood stirred and coursed through the veins of my soul. Without thinking, I uttered under my breath the ancient response: *Holy Mary, Mother of God, pray for us sinners...*

I suddenly understood the reason for all the cars—it was the Feast of the Assumption, a Catholic Holy Day. We had arrived at this shrine to Mary on her Feast Day completely by accident. I had forgotten the day because it is not observed as a Holy Day of Obligation in the Episcopal Church.

Isaac's attention turned quickly from walking Jackson. "I'm hot, Mom," he said, and tugged her hand. "Can I get something to drink?"

Wendy kept walking up the narrow paved path that went into the woods and answered, "Not right now, honey."

"What does he want?" Pappy asked from behind us.

"I'm hot Pappy, I want something to drink."

"Hey Buddy," I said, "We won't be here too long. Let's go say a prayer and then we'll get you something when we leave."

This shrine was one of my Mom's favorite places to visit. It had become a favorite of Wendy as well. It must have something to do with motherhood, I thought. I remembered having my picture taken when I was 11 or 12, standing behind the altar in the grotto. It was hewn into a rocky hillside and made to look like the one in Lourdes, France. It was one of those moments that you remember everything, like the smell of the candles burning and the sight of Mom sitting on a nearby bench, all branded into the memory of my soul the moment the shutter clicked. I had a light blue 1970's velour shirt, matching shorts, tube socks pulled to just below my knees and white Converse high–tops. Mom sat on the bench watching Dad take the photo. I was standing behind the altar just inside the little man–made cave. The soot on the walls and ceiling gave evidence to the years of prayers lit on the candles. When I stood behind the stone altar that day, I thought I'd be one who would always be standing behind an altar.

This place marked my soul.

It was our third trip to the grotto since we had been married and it was our first as Episcopalians. I was treading on ground that was all too familiar, but deep down I felt like a stranger.

We passed a little white chapel and a group of people who were singing and praying at each Station of the Cross, a Catholic prayer that took the believer along the route to Calvary, pausing for prayer at each of the 14 stations along the path. With Wendy watching, Isaac and I lit a candle and placed it on the stone shelf in the little cave; the scene gave me a sense of déjà vu.

We then picked a quiet place to hang out. Wendy went into the little chapel, and I took Isaac and Jackson over to a rock that was known as St. Elizabeth Seton's rock. We laid back on it and with our heads touching, watched the summer sky. "Look, Dad!" Isaac said. He pointed to the sky. "Look how the clouds are moving past us!"

"Yeah, pretty cool, huh?"

I remembered a cloud that Wendy and I had seen a couple weeks ago. For about 50 miles, the same cloud had stayed directly in front of us, as we drove the interstate. It never moved with the other clouds. It was shaped in the form of the Risen Christ—with His arms outstretched in blessing. The next day I got in the car and found a green scapular in the cup holder and hung it on the mirror. Wendy thought I had bought it; I thought she had. Years ago, after I was ordained a priest, a scapular had appeared in my briefcase. I believed that God had an angel put it there. Did an angel put this one in our car?

I briefly thought about the book Wendy was reading on Medjugorje, and how I had long ago tossed it in the garbage thinking it was nonsense. Now here I was on the Feast of the Assumption at a Marian Shrine.

"Dad! Dad! Are you sleeping?" I opened my eyes to find Isaac hovering over me—our noses were touching. "Dad...what are you doing? You've been laying on this rock too long."

"I'm just remembering."

"Oh...Can I walk Jackson?"

"Sure." I sat up and handed him the leash. "But first you need to give me a hug."

He ran and jumped up to hug me. "I love you, Dad."

"And I love you, Buddy!"

"Dad?"

"Yeah?"

"I'm really thirsty! Can we go and get a drink now?"

With that, I returned to the reality of the present.

CHAPTER XLI

After our vacation, I decided to read the Weible book, **Medjugorje: The Message.** Once I started reading it, I couldn't stop. I finished it in the middle of the night and immediately knew I had to go there.

If the author's life was so drastically changed, maybe the quiet yearnings I was feeling really were not that far off. Maybe the Virgin Mary really was calling me—calling *us* to Medjugorje. If this was real, and I believed it was, I wanted to put myself on God's ground and simply give thanks for Wendy's healing.

I had first heard as a teenager about the Virgin Mary appearing in apparition in Medjugorje to six Croatian kids who were close to my age. While in seminary, I once actually halfway made plans to go check it out, but the war broke out in Yugoslavia and my plans were cancelled. Now, years later after reading the book, I knew I had to go. I remembered Ephraim telling us that his gift of healing came to him while he was there. It suddenly seemed Medjugorje just wouldn't go away.

When Father Ephraim came to the parish for another healing service, he shared that he was going back to Medjugorje in a few months. It was now clear to us; we had to go with him. We wondered though, whether Isaac should go. After two weeks of praying the rosary together and fasting on bread and water, things the Virgin was asking us to do in her messages to the visionaries, we decided to take Isaac. After all, Mary is a mom, and she did appear to children.

We worried about the cost of the trip but the very next day, we received word that the check we had sent to pay for a kitchen counter top had been lost, and the company had not processed the order. Incredibly, the lost check was the exact amount, down to the dollar, for the cost of three pilgrims going to Medjugorje. I knew then, without hesitation, we were being called to go.

After we decided to go on the pilgrimage with Father Ephraim's group, I felt a tremendous sense of peace. With all the difficulties at St. Paul's, the upcoming pilgrimage could not have come at a better time. Every night we would gather in our bedroom and pray the rosary—Isaac lay in bed next to Wendy, while Pappy would sit on the sofa and I sat in a nearby chair. With every Hail Mary, I felt like I was falling in love with the Mother of God.

Not only did I feel as though Mary was mothering me, I believed she was also sending affirmations along the way, which seemed spiritually connected and always happened in the weirdest ways at the weirdest times.

One such weird event happened on our way back from a parish function. Wendy and I were listening to a book on tape, *Looking for Mary*, by Beverly Donofrio. Wendy had found the tape on the clearance table at Barnes and Noble. "I know you don't like religious books Michael, but this one sounded pretty neat. It's about a woman who collects statues of Mary and ends up going on a pilgrimage to Medjugorje as a reporter."

As we continued to listen, Wendy suddenly shrieked, "Michael, that's Ephraim Freed! She's talking about Father Ephraim!"

I hit the rewind button and turned up the volume. "No, it can't be Eph."

"Yes it is Michael! Listen!"

I gave her a look of disdain. "No way, come on. How many balding middle age priests are out there? She just described 80 percent of the clergy." I hit rewind again.

"There! Did you hear that? She said that he had little hands and feet. Plus she said that he was a retired science teacher. That's got to be Ephraim!"

I grabbed my cell phone and dialed Eph's number. "Hello, St. John's."

"Hello, is this the famous Father Freed from that book about Medjugorje?" I said, trying to disguise my voice.

There was a moment of silence, then Eph's classic snicker. "Rip?"

Strangely, as assured and confident as I was about making a pilgrimage to Medjugorje, a part of me was hesitant. I did not want to get caught up in some religious frenzy. Was the phenomena of Medjugorje a collective conscious event, born out of societal necessity—like the need to be freed from a tyrannical government and poverty? Were the Franciscans in the middle of a giant scam?

The skepticism would not leave me. Maybe the people there just wanted tourism and money. Some nights I was plagued with thoughts that I was going to nothing more than a giant hoax. The Church had let me down once before, I rationalized, and I knew the human side of the priests and bishops all too well.

There were other fears. I wouldn't experience the supernatural; I was afraid of being with staunch Roman Catholics, whose religious behavior had for unknown reasons always annoyed me; and, I was afraid of attending with people from my old Catholic diocese who might subject Wendy and even Isaac to criticism for what they saw as my sin of leaving the priesthood

However, the biggest issue was greater than all the fears and wonderings: I knew I was ex–communicated and that I would not be allowed to receive Holy Eucharist. In Mary's eyes…in her Son's eyes, was I even welcome in Medjugorje?

In the end, I went on nothing but faith.

CHAPTER XLII

I had come alone to the late–night adoration service in Saint James Church in Medjugorje, leaving Wendy and Isaac back in our tiny room preparing for bed. Despite my fears, there was no doubt I was called to this holy place through my dreams, my loves and my hope to offer a simple prayer of thanksgiving for Wendy's healing from cancer. There was no doubt we as a family were called to be here.

But this night, the night Pope John Paul II died, something stirred deep in my soul as I knelt on the marble in front of the con-fessionals. Primal memories of a faith abandoned long ago roused from their slumber. I knelt outside a sacred space once so familiar to me, outside a church where I once was a shepherd, where I was the one who sought to save the lost and sinful.

Now, I was the lost.

I slowly rose from my knees, looked up at the stars and began my walk back to where we were staying. I crossed the street and passed by a girl closing her souvenir stand. She wheeled the cart of rosaries back into the little store front and I noticed a black First

Holy Communion prayer book and rosary gift pack on the rack. It reminded me of my childhood prayer book.

Two young priests hustled past me towards the church, one fumbling to fix the white tab in his clerical shirt as he walked. I thought back of my early days of wearing that same collar, so defining of a Catholic priest. As I blankly stared in the window of the souvenir stand, the church bells begin tolling the death of the Holy Father.

I stepped into the road and car lights headed right for me. I jumped back onto the sidewalk; the Volkswagen sedan swerved away, honked, and then sped past me and up the hill. Great, I almost died the same night as the Pope, I thought.

Walking down the darkened side street lined with hedges and littered with papers and empty pop cans, I remembered I was going to turn 40 in two days. I would have thought it positively ludicrous if someone had told me 10 years ago that I would be celebrating my birthday with my wife and son halfway across the world, in a poor mountain village where Mary is appearing. I would have laughed right in his face.

Now, I chuckled to myself at the irony of realizing I had absolutely no control over anything whatsoever in my life. I am a man who is both free and afraid, I thought. For the first time in my life, I have a fear of the Lord.

I swallowed and felt little jagged spikes in my throat, as I opened the front door of the house where we were staying. I'm probably getting sick, I thought as I walked up the wide granite staircase and down the dark hallway to our room. Quietly, I opened the door and by the light of the moon through the open window, I made my way over to my bed. Each of us had our own little twin bed that sat just a few inches off the floor. I caught a glimpse of Isaac as he stirred and turned in his sleep.

"Michael?" Wendy whispered.

"Hey, it's me." I sat on the edge of my bed and untied my hiking boots.

"How was Adoration?"

"I got pushed out."

"What?"

"Nothing. I'll tell you in the morning. The pope died."

Wendy sat up. "Just now?"

"Yeah." I got up and walked over and gave Isaac a kiss before climbing into the little bed. Then I bent over and gave Wendy a kiss. "Good night. I love you."

"I love you, too," she whispered, as she flapped her sheets.

"Hot flash?"

"Yeah."

I lay in bed, wondering what she was thinking and how she was feeling. I wondered if she felt as out of sync and out of place as I did here. My wife was only a few feet away, but I missed her terribly.

I closed my eyes and pictured the scene from earlier in the day. We were at an apparition where Mary appeared to a visionary. Thousands of people had gathered inside and alongside a huge building that wasn't quite finished. People were standing, sitting and leaning on anything they could find. The veteran pilgrims brought little folding chairs. Some knelt in prayer and were experiencing their own ecstasy with arms outstretched and eyes rolled back. Others sat alone and prayed—their rosary beads dangling from their hands.

There were little children laughing and playing and babies asleep in backpacks. Cigarette smoke permeated the air. It was like a spiritual Woodstock. Between songs, people prayed the rosary simultaneously, responding in their native tongue. It was as if the Tower of Babel had just collapsed, and everyone was crying out to the Virgin to bring them back to God.

When we first arrived, I was granted admission to the reserved section for priests. This came about only after Wendy and one of our fellow pilgrims, a persistent Filipino woman from my old diocese, insisted that I go because, technically, I was still a priest.

As we approached the entrance, a teenage boy guarding the entrance said, "What? You have a wife and child? You are not a priest!" Giving me a sarcastic look, he shook his head and mumbled in English to his friend as he reluctantly allowed me to enter, "Must be an American thing!"

For a few moments I stood next to Ephraim in the balcony of the church, but I felt awful. The teenager was right. I didn't belong here. I was abusing a gift for nothing more than a good seat. I needed to be with Wendy and Isaac. My place in life was with them—not on some VIP balcony.

Deciding to leave the privileged balcony space, I nudged and prodded against the current of people swarming into the building. Once outside I searched for Wendy and Isaac and finally found them on a little hillside removed from the crowd. We claimed our spot, which looked directly into the open windows of the building.

The three of us responded in unison to the Hail Mary's over the loudspeaker. I remember the drone of the prayers; then, in an instant, there was complete silence nothing—as if a mother put her finger up to her lips, showing her children that they needed to be quiet and calm down.

I went to my knees.

After a few minutes, I heard a bird chirp in a nearby bush. Moments later, there was a gentle stirring of the crowd, as though everyone was waking up. Soon the music started, and then after a few minutes the translator shared the message. Mirjana, the visionary, spoke a few sentences in Croatian, which then were translated into Italian, German, and English.

The message from the Blessed Virgin given to Mirjana stated: *Renew my Church. Begin with your family. I will be with you always.*

I shifted position on the small bed and tilted my head to swallow around the pain. As I drifted off to sleep, I wondered if I was the one who was to renew the church like St. Francis, who was told by Christ in a vision to "rebuild my church". What did Mary mean? Did she mean it in some ecumenical way? Was I supposed to help renew the Episcopal and Anglican Church? What did she mean by "start with your family"? Were the Ripples supposed to be at the center of all of this? I didn't know what or how; all I knew was that some church somewhere had to be renewed and that the pope had died.

By morning, I was stricken mute and for the first time in my life. It was just as in Holy Scriptures when John the Baptist's father Zachariah was made mute because he questioned God's plan to enter into salvation history. His wife Elizabeth, who was well past childbearing age and whose womb was barren, was to give birth to John the Baptist. Zachariah questioned it, and the rest is history. Maybe Zachariah was my new patron saint.

I couldn't speak, so I had no choice but to listen.

The first 24 hours in Medjugorje had been eventful: we had a visit from Mary, the pope died, and I lost my voice. At least Isaac was having fun. My fear that people would judge Wendy and me never happened—thank God. The pilgrimage group was pretty cool; there were even a few other non–Catholics in the mix. The buzz at breakfast was about Pope John Paul. I overheard one table of pilgrims talking about hopping a ferry to Italy to go to the funeral.

Our guide, Ana, walked into the small dining hall, walked over to Isaac, and ruffled his hair. "Are you having fun, Izick?"

"Yes! I like how they eat breakfast here!"

Ana took a spoon and clinked it against the side of a glass. "My dear lovely group…"

Everyone got quiet as she added, "Let us say a prayer for our dear Holy Father." Together we prayed an Our Father, Hail Mary and Glory Be. Ana concluded by saying, "Eternal rest grant unto him, O' Lord."

We responded in unison, "And let perpetual light shine upon him."

"May his soul..." Ana said, then turned to Father Ephraim. "Father, how you say in English?"

"May his soul and all the souls of the faithfully departed rest in peace," Ephraim said.

"Amen."

Ana then gave us the itinerary for the day: "This morning, we will take taxis to Apparition Hill. After you climb the hill and pray, you can take taxi back to church for Holy Mass. The English Mass will be at 12 o'clock noon, so you want to make sure you are there early enough to get a seat. People will be pushing to get in. Catholics are sometimes too eager to get in church and forget manners," Ana said, chuckling.

Great...Mass, I thought. I knew it would be an issue. We could go, I muttered silently, but we better not get in line for Holy Communion; not because we didn't believe in the real presence of Jesus Christ, but because of man–made rules. Now, even in my thinking I was getting upset: What about all those people who continue to commit more heinous sins than Wendy and I—and never confess them? And yet, they continue to walk up the aisles in Roman Catholic churches throughout the world on any given Sunday receiving the Body of Christ.

What about priests who lead double lives? I had some double moments—but they have double lives. What about priests who live secret lives of sin and even those who publicly show a disregard for the church and a God they pledged to serve, and yet still consecrate and receive by their own hands every day? I simply knew and had experienced too much to just turn a blind eye and not feel hurt.

Hours later we were at the top of Apparition Hill. It was exactly as I had seen in the pictures—barren, brown and rocky. At the top was a statue of Mary standing where the first few days of apparitions occurred. After the group reached the top, everyone did their own spiritual thing. Some stood by the statue while others picked seats on nearby secluded rocks.

Wendy sat a little ways off, and I watched her as she took some photos. Isaac was having fun jumping from rock to rock and praying in his own little boy way.

Eventually we headed down the hill and walked towards the center of town, a few miles off. At some point, the dirt path ended and we were walking through a vineyard. I hoarsely whispered to Wendy and Isaac, "I have no idea which way to go."

"Are we lost?" Isaac asked.

"No," Wendy said, and then pointed ahead. "Michael, I can see the steeples of St. James over there." She removed the scarf from around her neck and tied it onto the shoulder strap of her purse.

"Yeah, it's getting warm," I said with my raspy voice and took a swig of water.

From my estimate, we were somewhere between the town of Medjugorje and Podbdro, generally known as Apparition Hill. I pointed to the steeples and with a throaty whisper said, "I say we keep walking in this direction."

"Good one, Dad," Isaac jeered.

"Yeah, Dad…good one," Wendy said, and smiled.

We were one hour early for the English Mass and we couldn't go inside St. James Church because the Germans were having their

Mass. The overflow of people attending were seated outside on the benches. We found some shade by the front steps and sat down, resting our backs against the cool stonewall of the church. Isaac traced the mortar joints with his finger, while over the loudspeakers you heard the priest giving his sermon in German.

The three of us said nothing as we stared blankly around and watched people, some praying, some talking and some taking pictures. I looked up again at the sun, which amazingly, was spinning. Every day since we arrived the sun had been spinning; not some little perimeter thing—but spinning and pulsating and looking like a communion host, a phenomenon quite common in Medjugorje, I learned.

A small commotion erupted, which meant the sign of peace was being exchanged during Mass. Then, within a matter of seconds, the ancient chant of the Agnus Dei, or Lamb of God, began. Three times it was chanted, and I uttered it under my breath, *Agnus Dei qui tollis peccata mundi miserere nobis. Agnus Dei qui tollis peccata mundi miserere nobis. Agnus Dei qui tollis peccata mundi dona nobis pacem.*

In my head, I went through the actions and the prayers that the priest would be doing at that moment inside St. James. Standing behind the altar and facing the congregation, he would break the Host apart, place a piece of it in the chalice, and say, "May this mingling of the body and blood of our Lord Jesus Christ bring eternal life to us who receive it." Then he'd bow and quietly say: "Lord Jesus Christ, with faith in your love and mercy, I eat your body and drink your blood. Let it not bring me condemnation, but health in mind and body." He would end the quiet prayers with a genuflection and then raise the broken Host for all to see, proclaiming: "This is the Lamb of God, who takes away the sins of the world. Happy are those called to receive Him."

I wanted to receive the Eucharist, but then thought, *No, I want us to receive the Eucharist.*

The side doors of the church opened and the priests who were helping with distributing Holy Communion came out and began. A priest came right over to us. "The Body of Christ," he said, placing the Host in Wendy's hands.

"Amen."

"The Body of Christ," he said, offering the Host to Isaac.

"Amen."

"The Body of Christ." It was now my turn.

"Amen."

Other than the times Isaac had received Communion from my hands as an Episcopal priest—this was officially the first time he received it in the context of the Roman Mass. Michael Isaac Ripple had just received his First Holy Communion—in Medjugorje.

On the way back to our house we stopped at one of the religious souvenir shops to buy a rosary for Isaac. It seemed like there were at least 500 of them in the village. He had his heart set on the color blue. From behind the register, the young woman keeping the store watched us search and offered some help.

"This one?" she asked in broken English, as she held out a blue rosary. It even came with its own special case, which was very cool to a little boy and, of course we bought it for him.

Back in our room, Isaac couldn't wait to open his prize. When he did, to our surprise the rosary and case were part of a First Holy Communion set that even included a lapel pin. It was another little sign; the place was full of them. Behind our smiles was wonderment and a question—really, what is going on here?

The next morning our group gathered once again at the base of Apparition Hill. We all were going to make a public consecration to the Immaculate Heart of Mary and receive a little brown scapular to hang around our necks. The first scapular I ever received was at my First Holy Communion. It had a picture of the Blessed Virgin handing the scapular to St. Simon Stock. I never knew his story, and I remember wanting to have something like that happen to me—where Mary or God would directly tell me what to do.

We all said our prayers then walked part way up the hill to where a small blue metal cross stood. John, the leader of the group, who was hoping to find a good Catholic wife on one of his trips here, asked Isaac to place a bouquet of flowers at the little concrete statue of Mary beside the metal cross. Wendy and I sat on a stone bench and watched as Isaac placed the flowers. Wendy was snapping a picture just as Isaac's little hands brushed against the banner that was carved on the base of the statue. She pulled the camera away, stunned.

We turned and looked at each other in disbelief. Carved into the concrete banner were the letters MIR. Instantly, my dream from years ago of a visit from an angel, came to mind. The angel had told me to name my son Michael. Months later, Isaac was baptized—Michael Isaac Ripple—M.I.R., which in the Slavic language meant, Peace. In my way of thinking, God named our child. He named him after the title of His mother, Kraljica Mira, which is Croatian for Queen of Peace. I immediately knew it was important for me to see this sign.

I suddenly remembered there was another 'sign' that had occurred during our ride from Dubrovnik Airport to Medjugorje on the first day of our arrival. Wendy literally shocked me by asking completely out of the blue if maybe I should return to the Roman Catholic priesthood. I was dismayed and couldn't believe she had asked that. I loved my wife and son and would never want to lose them to go back to being a priest and I told her so emphatically.

Wendy had not mentioned it again but deep within my soul, I knew it was now connected with the sign about Isaac's name, as well as all of the other little signs.

Something was definitely going on beyond my understanding.

CHAPTER XLIII

My interpretation of the sign about Isaac's name confirmed for me that Wendy and I were supposed to be married and that our lives did have spiritual significance. There was no way that my subconscious would be creating these connections. Wendy and I being together, loving each other and having Isaac—all of this was good. We knew God had been with us. Yet, we both seemed to be simultaneously out of sorts. It had to be coming from something else, but what?

The next day, we began our morning trek, led like sheep up the dusty road to the Oasis of Peace, where a community of male and female consecrated religious spend their days and nights in communal and silent prayer. Situated in the center of their monastic compound was a chapel for perpetual Eucharistic Adoration; twenty–four hours a day, seven days a week, the Body of Christ is exposed, adored, and venerated by the community and pilgrims from all ends of the earth.

Isaac, Wendy and I walked inside the chapel, genuflected, and grabbed a spot in one of the 10 little pews. I looked at the Host in a

tabernacle that appeared to be hewn into the stone wall of the chapel, like a little sacred cave. The door of the tabernacle was open
revealing the Body of Christ.

We had spent the last few days surrounded by supernatural
spiritual phenomena. We watched the spinning sun, our rosaries
turned gold, images appeared in rocks and we had even wiped fluid
from a weeping statue of the Risen Christ. But those things didn't
settle me.

As I knelt in the pew before the Blessed Sacrament, I felt
something begin to rise up from deep within; it was like a small,
black pin hole in my heart slowly opening—revealing at that moment nothing but emptiness. I was terrified, and even more so,
ashamed, just as Peter had been when he denied knowing Jesus
Christ.

You were with him! No. No I wasn't! I don't even know the man!

After a few minutes, people from our group started to leave. I
had a feeling I was supposed to stay, but Wendy had a terrible migraine and there was no way I could hang out here while she kept
Isaac occupied for the rest of the day. Then Wendy leaned into me
and whispered, "You stay, I'll take Isaac back and we'll hang out at
the house. We'll come back later this evening for the apparition."

"No, that's alright, I'll go with you."

Wendy looked directly into my eyes and said with conviction,
"No, you need to be here, Michael. You stay—we'll be fine."

Somehow knowing she was right, I knelt down and right in
front of me was a life–size crucifix. Christ's body was dirty and
sweaty, and His wounds were open and bleeding. His hair and

beard were matted with blood, and the crown—the crown of thorns—dripped blood down His brow. It reminded me of that moment in college when I actually felt the thorns. For a moment, my hands, feet, head, and side felt them all, all of His wounds.

Take this all of you and eat. This is my Body, which is given up for you...

Behind the crucifix was a stained–glass window of St. Michael, thrusting a sword into the serpent, Satan. It was the Archangel Michael—the defender of God and the Church—who did battle against Lucifer and his army of demon angels, casting them into the bowels of Hell. He was my namesake; my mother had told me she chose my name so I would have the best archangel to protect me.

Can you drink of the cup I drink?

Hours later, Wendy and Isaac returned with the rest of the group. They slid quietly into the pew beside me and handed me a piece of crusty bread. Word must have spread through the village that there would be a private apparition by the visionary Marija at Oasis of Peace, because the place was quickly filling up with people. Two German women squeezed in beside us. People hung on the ledges of the open windows—just to catch a glimpse inside.

We must have prayed three rosaries in four different languages. It reminded me of Pentecost, all of us in one little space—like the upper room. Eventually we gave up our pew space and moved to the two–foot–wide side aisle. The German woman handed Isaac a little medal and smiled, thanking us for giving them room. Soon the visionary Marija arrived, walked up the center aisle, knelt down at the foot of the altar and began reciting the rosary with us.

At that point, Isaac reached his limit. He became bored and antsy and just wanted to leave. I couldn't blame him. I was preparing to take him outside in order to give Wendy some time alone, when all of a sudden there was complete silence. It was just like at the apparition a couple of days ago—total silence.

Wendy, kneeling just behind me, tapped my shoulder. I turned and saw Isaac completely out, laying back in his mother's arms—resting in the Holy Spirit. Wendy had tears streaming down her cheeks and I began to cry shaking my head and thinking, MIR.

Afterwards, as we stood outside the chapel, I asked Isaac, "Hey buddy, what happened in there?"

"I don't know. All I felt was someone push me on the forehead."

Wendy winked at me and said, "You know, on our way here Isaac asked me if I would 'concentrate' him to the Blessed Virgin Mary."

I shook my head in amazement. My son.

Following dinner at the house, we retired to our room where I crashed on my bed. Isaac lined up his rosaries, medals and holy cards. Wendy began pacing around. Her whole demeanor had changed. Her eyes were glaring and she had deep furrows in her forehead and I knew she was in a spiritual agony. There was nothing I could do to help her, because I was feeling the same.

Here we were surrounded and enveloped by God in this place and at this time; and still, we were lost, out of sync, spiritually disturbed and full of angst. Wendy looked at me and coarsely whispered, "It would be easier not to believe!"

I didn't know what to say to her.

At that moment Ephraim knocked on our door. "You ready, Wendy?"

I had forgotten that Wendy had scheduled time with Ephraim to go to confession. A few weeks earlier, before we left for the pilgrimage, she began writing her examination of conscience. She went over her entire life, naming her sins and faults and praying for God's forgiveness and grace. It was a spiritual exercise I truly admired.

At this point in our pilgrimage, Ephraim's timing wasn't much of a surprise. Wendy left the room and Isaac sat next to me on the bed, playing with a Lego robot. "Dad, where did Mom go?"

"She went to confession, buddy." I stretched out on the bed and Isaac snuggled beside me. I stared at the ceiling as he made robot noises with the toy.

"Dad, I want to go to confession too."

"Someday buddy, someday."

Early the next morning, I knocked on Ephraim's door. "You got a minute?"

"Sure, Rip." It was as if he was expecting me.

The bus for Tihaljina was leaving in 10 minutes. It was a small town about 25 miles from Medjugorje and where one of the most beautiful statues of the Virgin was located. We gathered our stuff and headed down the steps where the group was congregating on the patio in front of the house. Some people had already gotten on the bus to reserve their favorite seats.

Isaac went outside and teased his new friend, Mario, an old Italian man, who smoked his pipe, enjoyed his wine and called things and people the way he saw them. Mario was yelling at Isaac, "Okay, dog—you're the man, Isaac. You stick with old Mario."

Wendy stood next to me at the front door and together we just took it in. I could tell that she was in a much better frame of mind than she was last night. She seemed totally at peace. We didn't talk about her confession and she was not aware that I went that morning. She looked at me with a slight smile and asked, "You okay?"

That did it. My emotions flooded to the surface and I slowly nodded, "No."

Lightly touching her arm, I led her into the empty dining room well out of earshot and sight of the rest of the group. Wendy looked at me, puzzled, as she asked, "What's wrong, Michael?"

I looked in her eyes and paused. I was so nervous—more nervous than the first time I told her I loved her. She looked at me, waiting, with brown eyes so deep, so beautiful and so loving. I tightened my lips in order to keep from crying.

"Michael...?" She reached out and gently rubbed my arm.

I couldn't find the right words or the right order, but I had to tell her and it had to be right now, after my confession. Suddenly, Wendy hugged me and softly said, "Michael, I know."

She knew my heart and I felt it. Her heart was telling her the same. I knew then and there what I was feeling and thinking was definitely from the Holy Spirit of God. I blurted, "I...we...need to return to the Catholic Church, for the sake of our souls."

"Yes, I know," she said again, "I confessed last night."

"And I just went to Eph this morning. I confessed leaving the church, not being a good priest and husband and father...I confessed everything."

The look in her eyes conveyed all I desperately needed to hear. "It's alright Michael, I love you." She kissed the tears on my cheek.

the Return

2005–2006

"But to the penitent he provides a way back, he encourages those who are losing hope."
—from the Book of Sirach.

CHAPTER XLIV

Life was simple in Medjugorje. We prayed, we ate, and we surrendered to God. There were no distractions to get in the way. The reentry to daily life, on the other hand, was difficult.

We began to question our call to return to the Roman Catholic Church almost immediately as we left the little village of Medjugorje. Would God really expect us to just up and follow Him back on the original course? After all, the Episcopal faith had sheltered us, when we needed it most. Our rationalization continued to dominate our thoughts.

Every night, we had the same conversation about our direction. We didn't know what to do. The whole idea seemed crazy, but we couldn't escape the fact that we had both felt we were supposed to return.

We examined our options: We could stay where we were, which would be the easiest plan; or, we could return to the Roman Catholic Church, which would require me to repay a huge loan back to the Episcopal church, find a new job and lose a great deal of money along the way. It seemed an easy choice.

Adding to the negatives of returning to the Catholic faith, Wendy would also have to pursue the annulment process for her first marriage, a process she had started years ago and abandoned in disgust. Further complicating the issue, Wendy was under contract negotiations to work at a new practice in which one of the physicians was not only a part–time Episcopal priest, but my assistant at St. Paul's. It was a working relationship we feared would be jeopardized by our decision.

We thought of a third option: We could renew the church by becoming more Anglo–Catholic.

We kept coming back to questioning why God would want us to sell our house, uproot our family, and go deeper into debt just so we could return to the Roman Catholic Church—a church I still felt deep in my heart, didn't want us.

Two things happened that made us believe we were to stay Episcopal: The election of a new Catholic pope, and our meeting with the Episcopal bishop. Much to my dismay, the Catholic College of Cardinals elected Cardinal Joseph Ratzinger, who took the name Benedict XVI, as the new Roman Catholic pope. He was the man I had criticized during my time in seminary for his conservative views. I did not know how we would fit in under his papacy or even if we would be welcomed back.

Still, we didn't fit into the mindset and culture at St. Paul Episcopal Church. I didn't have the patience to be the pastor they wanted. Just a day before, a parishioner had sent me a letter suggesting that my preaching was too harsh and the words I used like 'sin' and 'sacrifice' were archaic and uncomfortable. The writer suggested I focus more on 'building people up.'

We decided we needed to find a niche in the Anglican tradition that allowed for the Virgin Mary and Eucharist. This would be the way we would renew the church. Wendy and I simply needed to find a more "Catholic" Episcopal Church.

That led to a meeting with Episcopal Bishop Wilson. The three of us met for a lunchtime chat. Wendy and I shared our experience of Medjugorje, including some of the small signs and miracles. We explained how we both felt the call to return to the Catholic faith independently of each other.

The bishop uncomfortably shifted his weight, played with his pectoral cross and looked right past us out of the window. "You're Episcopal, trust me, I know the two of you and you guys are Episcopal."

"Well, that's what we were thinking—but it just isn't working out," I said.

"Look, you're just having a bad go at St. Paul's," the bishop continued, hoping to find something positive. "I knew it was going to be tough. They've been set in their ways for years out there."

It was clear the bishop didn't want to talk about Medjugorje or our experience. What he wanted to do was fix my problem of being the rector at St. Paul's. "What you need is a ministry review," he said. "That will give you guys some peace."

A ministry review is a written survey completed by the entire parish, which gives everyone the chance to share views about the life, ministry, and worship of the parish community. In an ideal world a review is a great tool; it can, however, be used as an anonymous forum to rail against the minister.

The bishop set the wheels in motion for the review. Meanwhile, true to our call to renew the church, we invited the parish over to our house to share our experience of Medjugorje, and encouraged all to let Mary take their hands and put them into her Son's hand. We offered rosaries and scapulars to everyone in our home that night. The next day, Wendy started planning our second pilgrimage to Medjugorje. This one would be ecumenical. Father Ephraim liked the idea and agreed to go along.

We prayed, we fasted, we planned another pilgrimage and we began the process of a ministry review. But, as the weeks progressed, we found no peace. Life at St. Paul's became even more difficult and the gossip and opinions even more spiteful. Was this the devil? Would all the crap stop if we just ignored what happened to us in Medjugorje?

We decided to call Bishop Hoffman, the Roman Catholic bishop of the local diocese. He knew who I was and was quick to schedule some time for Wendy and me. It seemed much too easy.

The bishop's secretary greeted us and ushered us into the waiting room. Wendy sat patiently on the couch, while I paced around the room. I felt so out of place and out of sorts; I never imagined myself as a prodigal son and Bishop Hoffman really had no reason to help us. The last time I met with him was when the Episcopal bishop had arranged for the three of us to meet as protocol and good ecumenical relations.

Bishop Hoffman walked into the waiting room, smiled broadly and extended his hand, "Hello Wendy! Hello Michael! Come, come, right this way!"

Wendy and I sat opposite his desk while he listened intently to our story, nodding his head and urging us on. The space surrounding us seemed to become spiritually charged. Wendy and I shared everything from how we met years back to our marriage by a Justice of the Peace, to Isaac, to the Episcopal Church, to cancer, to Medjugorje and the Blessed Virgin Mary. At the end of our abbreviated biography, we spontaneously said in unison: "We want to return to the Roman Catholic Church!"

The bishop pushed his chair back, stood up slowly, came around his desk and embraced us. "Welcome home!" he said with a broad smile.

I could not believe what was happening.

We all sat back down and the bishop directed the conversation to our future, for which he seemed genuinely concerned. "Now Wendy, I know you'll keep being a doctor, but Michael, what will you do?" How will you help to provide for your family? Will you go back to being a therapist?"

"Well, Bishop, if it's possible I'd like to somehow work in the Church, but I'm not sure what I am allowed to do."

"Yes, I know there are certain restrictions—but we can work something out. God wouldn't be calling the two of you to come back if He wasn't going to provide!"

As the bishop walked across the hallway to find the vicar general of the diocese, I glanced at Wendy and gave her a wink. She was beaming. He came back with the vicar general and together the four of us talked about what our next steps would be for us to return. Wendy would begin to work on an annulment, and I would begin on a petition to Rome.

The petition involved gathering past information, from my early family life, to seminary formation, to ordained ministry, and eventually to getting married and leaving the Church. I would need a recorded interview and letters written by people supporting my case—saying I should be released from the promise of celibacy and the daily praying of the Liturgy of the Hours. The process would take about a year for Wendy's annulment and two or three for mine, all dependent upon Rome.

The bishop encouraged me to continue as the rector at St. Paul's Episcopal until I was ready to send my petition and appeal my case to the Vatican. He was well aware of our financial concerns if I quit. He then led us to the Tribunal Office to make sure everything was set in motion.

My double life began; I was now an active Episcopal priest seeking to return to the Catholic Faith and Church where I had been baptized. There was a deep pervading sense of spiritual peace. We knew we were on the right road. But the road was certainly rough. It was filled with the strains and worries of impending unemployment and debt. In addition, the day–to–day pastoral responsibilities at St. Paul's continued with their challenges.

I put myself where I needed to be next to the Eucharist. Like some double agent, I started frequenting Roman Catholic tabernacles situated throughout the city. I started spending more time at the hospitals after making rounds simply because they had the Holy Eucharist reserved in their chapel tabernacles. On other days, I'd lose the collar and sit anonymously in a Catholic Church.

On one occasion, Wendy met me in the afternoon at St. Joseph's Roman Catholic Cathedral for First Friday Devotions and confession. Even though I went to confession in Medjugorje, I knew that according to church law, I wasn't able to receive absolution or any of the sacraments because I was excommunicated. I glanced and saw the little red light shine above the door to the confessional—Wendy was in.

The door of the confessional opened and out walked Wendy with a huge smile. Right behind her was Monsignor Rosenbaum. He was making a beeline for me. He shook his finger at me in the air and motioned for me to wait. He turned to those waiting in line and assured them he would be back in a minute. The people must have thought, "My God, what did that man do? What did that woman confess?"

In a small alcove away from the confessionals, Monsignor Rosenbaum hugged me and whispered, "Welcome home! Oh, my brother, I've been praying for you! This is terrific!"

There were days when I didn't think it was so terrific. Those days usually centered on the demon trying to get in and just mess everything up. Maybe it couldn't stop us from returning to Rome, but it sure could make our lives miserable

Even though I would eventually be leaving, I still needed to be the pastor, and this particular Sunday I had to address a divisive issue in the congregation—gossip. Following the reading from the

Gospel, the people sat down in their pews. "I'll be right back," I said, and I walked into a little alcove off to the side of the front of the church.

I reappeared carrying a portable wooden podium and set it in the center aisle between the first two pews. I folded my arms underneath my green chasuble and alb. Slowly and deliberately I looked in the eyes of most of the members of the congregation.

"I apologize to any visitors who are with us this morning, but I need to take care of some spiritual housekeeping. Some of you— and you know who you are—will not like what I am about to say. There may be some of you who will like what I have to say. And then there will be some of you who will remain indifferent."

I continued, "There are some people from this congregation saying that Wendy's cancer has returned. What is interesting is that it has come from people who are actually feigning care and concern about my wife. These are the same people who basically can't stand that I am a priest here at St. Paul's. Do you think this is a coincidence? Nobody asked me or called me, or even Wendy, to verify these rumors. What if someone came up to my son and said, 'Gee, I'm sorry that your Mom's cancer came back'?"

I had a burst of spiritual strength. "These behaviors and all the other gossiping, rumor mongering and sabotaging are demonic and evil."

As I continued preaching a woman named Francine stood up, huffed and slung her purse over her shoulder. She did the sideways shuffle and tried to get out of the pew as fast as possible and then stormed to the back of the church. Following the closing hymn the doors opened, and there she was, waiting for me. Francine interrupted the first person who was on their way out and was shaking my hand. "You are wrong!" she hollered over the person's shoulder, pointing her finger in my face.

"Francine, I'm through with you and your ways. This is over."

"Oh, you think it's over? It isn't! Who do you think you are? You're nothing. You have to listen to me! I pay you!"

I grabbed some people from the vestry for witnesses, and together with Wendy, we went into my office. I wanted to quit right there on the spot. This wasn't worth it. Wendy had tears in her eyes and the others just sat there in disbelief. At one point in her tirade, Francine yelled, "Eucharist, Eucharist, Eucharist! I feel like I'm being inundated with Eucharist!"

That said it all.

At home, I was mixing a gin and tonic when the phone rang. Francine had been admitted to the hospital with chest pains. I hung up the phone and slammed my hands down on the kitchen table. "Would you believe that?" I turned and looked at Wendy with my hands turned upward. "This is crazy! If she dies, you know I'm the one who's to blame! This just keeps getting better!"

"You have to go Michael, Wendy said as she placed her hand on my arm. "If you don't, then everyone will hear about it. If you do, then she won't tell anyone and at least you did what you were supposed to do as a priest. And who knows, maybe there will be a healing."

At the hospital I stopped at the nurse's station. "Would you let the patient know that Father Michael is here and was wondering if she wanted to be anointed and receive Holy Eucharist?"

The nurse came out of the room shaking her head, no.

CHAPTER XLV

My sermon was dubbed the "kick–ass sermon" by a few supportive parishioners. I saw it as a way to move forward beyond the mire of opinions and criticism. In some ways, knowing I planned to leave allowed me to revise my vision for the parish, removing agendas that caused so much anxiety and frustration. For some, this was probably seen as a victory; I could only imagine how happy they must have been to see the 'For Sale' sign go up in our front yard.

The Episcopal bishop called me to ask about the sign. I did tell the truth, though I chose to leave out a few particulars. I told him we were downsizing, which was true; I just didn't mention we needed to downsize because I would soon be facing unemployment.

It was a good purging for us. We packed all of our necessities in boxes and stacked them in our prayer room. Everything else that wasn't deemed necessary was sold at our first–ever garage sale. During our free time, we cruised neighborhoods to look for a new home.

Every week our pilgrimage group would meet at St. Paul's. At our first meeting, Wendy and I talked about the Virgin Mary and how she is viewed in the Anglican and Episcopal tradition. I even referred to the revival of the so–called Anglican prayer beads as nothing more than a rosary. As I outlined all the theology and spirituality surrounding the prayers and history of Marian devotion, someone finally said, "We get it, Michael, you don't have to defend it; we believe!"

Without any hesitation Wendy said, "Then let's pray the rosary together." Every one of them reached into their pockets or purses and pulled one out! Thus, for a few short months, St. Paul's Episcopal Church had a Marian prayer group. It was a blessing from Mary that helped us navigate a difficult time.

We continued to make progress on our return to the Catholic Faith. Three months after filing the paperwork, we received notice about Wendy's annulment. I was looking through the mail and saw something from the diocese, but figured that it was just another form that needed to be completed. Wendy opened it. "This is it!" She did a happy dance.

"What?"

"This is my annulment. Here, look!"

I quickly read it. "Uh, oh…."

"What?" she asked and stopped dancing.

"It says here that you should consider seeking counsel before entering into another union. That means you need to see a shrink before getting married to me!"

"Well, they must know you," she quipped and gave me a quick kiss.

Things were moving faster than expected. The next step was to send my petition to Rome, which couldn't be done until I had officially resigned from my position as rector and left the Episcopal tradition. Now, the question became one of timing. If I resigned immediately, I would be unemployed, we would lose a big chunk of our income, I would lose my pension and we would be in debt to the Episcopal church.

More importantly, there was something in me that wanted to share our journey of return in a better light. I wanted to share it for the people who still considered me their priest. Maybe just maybe, our journey would encourage others to pursue whatever reconciliation needed to happen in their lives. I decided to write a letter of resignation from the Episcopal priesthood.

Wendy and I met again with Episcopal Bishop Wilson. I explained to him that the review had gone badly. The responders had assailed me, Wendy and even Isaac; my father was the only one who had escaped their criticism. It was nothing more than a setup, I told the bishop; it was clear the people did not want me and that I had decided to resign and renounce the priesthood effective in six months.

Bishop Wilson refused to take my letter of resignation and did not want to listen to me, saying he knew the priesthood was in me and that I could not leave. I sensed that he did not want to go deeper into the faith issues that we had been examining. Instead, the bishop offered a quick solution; ironically, he advised me to see a Roman Catholic priest counselor. He was certain that after counseling, he could find a place for me to work as an Episcopal priest.

Bishop Wilson did not want to hear anymore. He left it at that and departed for a three–month sabbatical. Shortly after the meeting, we left for our second pilgrimage to Medjugorje.

For some reason during our first pilgrimage to Medjugorje, we were not able to visit Father Jozo Zovko, a Franciscan priest who had laid his hands on Father Ephraim during a pilgrimage in the 1990s. Afterwards, Ephraim became an instrument of God's healing. On this trip, we would be able to hear his story.

Father Jozo had been the pastor of St. James Church in Medjugorje when the apparitions began. He was later imprisoned, brutally beaten and kept in solitary confinement by the Communist government of Yugoslavia. The charge was treason, because of words he had used in a sermon that the authorities took as an attack on Communism. It was also his refusal to stop the gatherings of the people in Medjugorje for the evening prayers and the apparition.

After his release, Father Jozo was transferred to a Franciscan monastery in Siroki Brijeg, located about 25 miles from Medjugorje. In 1948, a large number of Franciscans had been doused with fuel, set afire and martyred by the Communists on the church grounds. It was a place of holy blood.

There were about 70 pilgrims seated in the little auditorium in Siroki Brijeg, as Father Jozo shared his teaching and catechesis. He was a tall man with a wisp of dark hair and soft eyes. It was those eyes, however, that locked with mine as he spoke something in Croatian. He continued to stare at me, as the translator shared his last comment: "The Anglicans think they have Eucharist—but they don't."

I wasn't dressed as a priest. How did Father Jozo know?

We were asked to stay in our seats. Father Jozo would be around to give each of us his blessing. He stood before me, Wendy and Isaac, who now was asleep in his mother's arms. He placed his right hand on Wendy, his left on me, and then gently touched Isaac. He made the sign of the cross over us, as a family, and moved on to the next person. As we stood to leave, I glanced over at him, and once again our eyes met.

I whispered to Wendy, "I have to stay. I think he wants to talk to me."

Father Jozo continued to make his way to the back of the auditorium, aisle by aisle. He looked over at me, standing along the side wall, and motioned for me to have a seat to wait. Just then, our guide Slavenka walked past. I asked her to translate when Father Jozo talked with me.

"Are you sure? He usually doesn't talk with anyone," she said.

Right at that moment, Father Jozo came over. I stood and extended my hand. "Father Jozo, I'm..."

"Yes, Michael..."

He kept hold of my hand and led me down to the front of the room, which was now completely empty. He pulled a chair over and motioned for Slavenka to have a seat with us.

"You are a priest, I know…and you left the priesthood…and you are now Anglican…and you are coming back."

I started to cry—actually sob. We didn't need anything translated. I understood everything perfectly. He told me about how I had a difficult time as a young priest and even though I left and became Episcopalian, God knew I was trying to be a good father and husband, and even a good priest.

"And you are coming back to the Church where you belong. You will continue to share the priesthood. Yes, it is hard right now. But do not be afraid. Everything will work out."

He placed his hands on my head and said, "Her mantle is covering you."

CHAPTER XLVI

God gives you just enough. His timing is always perfect. We returned home just before Advent and Christmas.

Wendy and I had just finished wrapping and hiding Christmas presents and were getting ready for bed. Isaac was already asleep in his special set up of sleeping bags and blankets he put together on the couch in our room. The telephone rang. "Who would be calling us this late?" Wendy said, pulling the comforter back and climbing in bed.

"Take a guess!" I said. I read the phone number and name on the caller ID and felt nauseated; it was the Episcopal bishop. "You've got to be kidding me! It's after 11 o'clock!"

Wendy looked at me. "You have to answer it."

"No way, I don't want it tonight."

Once he had called late at night complaining he and his wife did not feel welcome at St. Paul's. I felt like saying, "Welcome to the club."

"Michael—answer it!"

"Hello?"

"Michael, this is the Bishop." Whenever he used his title, I knew he meant business. "Yes, good evening, Bishop."

"We just returned from the club where we were having cocktails with some of your parishioners." I remained silent.

"I want to talk to you about what is really going on at St. Paul's. What time are you available tomorrow?"

"Tomorrow?" Couldn't this wait until after Christmas? Tomorrow was December 23.

"Yes, tomorrow," he said, tersely.

Unfortunately, I was available and deep down, I knew this was the way it had to happen. I managed to muster a decent response and said, "Nine o'clock?"

"That would be fine. We'll meet at my house. Good night."

"Good night, Bishop." I kept talking into the receive after he hung up: "Sweet dreams, Bishop—hope you're happy—hope the club was fun—oh, and thanks for ruining Christmas. Good night, Bishop Grinch."

He really wasn't a grinch. I was just annoyed.

I hung up the phone, walked over to the fireplace and slid open the chain link screen. I picked up a log and threw it on the glowing embers. "We meet tomorrow at his house."

I crawled into bed, and Wendy nestled next to me. "It'll be fine. Just put it in Mary's hands."

I needed her confidence.

Watching the light from the fire dance off the ceiling and walls, I knew it had begun. Here we were getting ready to celebrate the Incarnation. It felt more like we were entering into the Passion and

Death of Jesus Christ. Wendy began praying the rosary aloud and it struck me—the shortest day of the year, the light breaking in and scattering the darkness, the birth of Christ, the birth of the Way and the Truth. Tomorrow would be my day of truth. There was no turning back.

The next morning, I made the short drive to the bishop's house. Everything looked so pure, bright and pristine. I pulled into the driveway and felt nauseated. My heart raced as I rang the doorbell. The bishop opened the door and said, "Michael, come in."

I made some small talk, but the bishop was not in the mood. He looked tired and sleepy and impatient. I followed him through the entrance hall, past the kitchen island and down a couple of steps into a sunken family room. The usual Christmas decorations were carefully arranged. He motioned for me to have a seat opposite him and got right into it. "So, tell me. What's going on?"

I crossed my legs and tried to pace my breathing. I touched the rosary in my front jeans pocket. "Look, I don't want to get into all the particulars and personalities. You and your wife have experienced what can happen at St. Paul's. Remember when you called me the one night because you guys didn't feel welcome?" He shook his head in agreement. "But that isn't what this is about any more. My moving to another parish is not the solution. Bishop, I didn't want this to end this way."

Bishop Wilson just stared at me. He had to know what was coming.

"You know it's much deeper." I uncrossed my legs and leaned forward. "Wendy, Isaac and I are returning to the Roman Catholic

Church. Wendy has already received her annulment, and I am in the process of asking the Pope to release me from my ordination promises. This is about the salvation of our souls. We need to do this."

He cleared his throat and forced a smile. I hit something so deep and so fundamental to his existence. For a split second, I knew he was thinking about his own journey when he left the Romans—but only for a split second.

"Well, then," the bishop said slowly, "I guess I will accept your resignation early."

I sat back in the chair and felt instant relief and fear.

"So, I'm fired, right?" Actually, the humor helped.

We chatted just a little more and then I received one of the greatest compliments in my life, "Michael, you're more a priest than I've seen in the majority of priests, Anglican and Roman."

I got in the car, drove to the end of the street and sat at the intersection. The momentary relief I felt was replaced with anxiety. We had just lost half our income and my pension, and now we owed a large debt to a church whose congregation couldn't stand me.

About 30 hours later, I held Isaac's hand and followed Wendy. We made our way through the crowd. We passed children dressed in their fuzzy red, white and green Christmas outfits and finally came to a space that seemed like it could fit us. It was almost as if the space had been reserved for us, as if Mary knew we would be arriving late for Christmas Eve Mass at a Catholic church. Isaac took a seat on the kneeler in front of the votive candle stand. I looked up past the candles and saw her staring at us—a statue of the Virgin Mary, Our Lady of Peace.

At the sign of peace, Wendy kissed me and whispered, "My prayer was answered."

"What prayer?"

"I prayed that we would go to Christmas Mass as a family."

Then, as the people filed up to receive Holy Eucharist, I stayed behind, taking comfort in the prayer that we just recited: "Lord, I am not worthy to receive you. Only say the word and I shall be healed."

Now I just needed to wait for the word.

CHAPTER XLVII

"Make him look like a funeral director," Wendy said to the man at the Men's Warehouse store, who was laying out different shirts and ties on a wide wooden table. He continued to take my measurements. "I have a few of the guys who come in from a couple of the homes in town—which one you with?"

The question nudged me into a surreal moment. Could I really be entering this new reality? This man, who was measuring me for a suit, knew me as nothing more than a funeral director. I had no past and no future—just the now. I was nothing more than a middle–aged, mildly obese guy with a slightly receding hairline, who was in the death business. He didn't know that I had been offered this job on the Feast of the Immaculate Conception, when I was working at St. Paul's Episcopal Church.

I was still trying to make sense of all that had happened including this new job; I continued the conversation with myself: Maybe the real cost of following Jesus is that my life needs to be totally reordered and that God needs to create order out of the chaos that

I made. I need to let go of my ego. I simply need to thank God for His Mother who took my heart and gave it back to Jesus.

So I let go. I stopped my soliloquy, and decided to buy the suits. It wasn't all bad, I rationalized; the second suit was half off. Maybe the death business would suit me, no pun intended.

I then entered a completely different world. I would drop Isaac at school, grab a coffee at the nearby Country Fair, and make it just in time for the morning staff meeting. For the first few weeks, I watched videos of how to exceed other people's expectations. I learned that the death business was nothing more than making sure the bereaved were satisfied, happy and content. I had to develop a personal mission statement that I'd share when I met the grieving party for the very first time. We would sit and plan the next couple of days, the viewing, the funeral and the flowers, while two flights down in the basement the corpse was being made to look like he or she was asleep.

Eventually I would lead them across the hall to another room where we would shop for a coffin and a burial vault. While I was truly grateful for the work—every day I said thank you to Mary—I kept trying to find some meaning.

Death was around every day. I was traveling to pick up bodies—all kinds, all shapes, all sizes: people stuck in upstairs apartments, people dead from AIDS, people hit by 18 wheelers and people long ago forgotten in subpar nursing homes. I moved $200 flower arrangements from beside a casket to the dumpster in a matter of hours. I chauffeured people who suddenly grew rude because all of a sudden they felt entitled.

I attended Mass during my lunch break.

In the meantime, our house sold, but there was a contingency clause dependent on the sale of the buyer's home. We were packed and stacked in boxes, waiting for the signal to move.

In the midst of all this, Isaac would soon be making his first *official* Holy Communion. Even though my petition was not even ready to be sent to the Vatican, I was hoping there was a way I would be able to receive; I called an old seminary classmate familiar with Canon Law. Wendy and I met with him in his office at the Chancery as he explained the reasoning why my hunch was right. It was not because I had left the Roman Catholic priesthood that I could not receive Eucharist. It wasn't even because Wendy and I had married. My spiritual insight, or hunch, would not let me receive the Body of Christ because I had made a *conscious* decision to renounce the faith of the Roman Catholic Church.

I had consciously excommunicated myself. I was outside of the Communion and my spiritual intuition that I wasn't yet worthy to share in that unifying act of God with humanity—His Body and Blood—was correct.

"Unfortunately, we do not have anyone in the diocese that has been given the authority to lift the type of excommunication you received because we never needed it," he explained after pausing briefly. "But we will have someone by five o'clock tonight."

I was numb with the thought that I might actually begin to receive Eucharist again.

The next day, I met with Monsignor Rosenbaum. In the emptiness and silence of the Cathedral, I received absolution and was set free from my excommunication. Following confession, the two of us walked over to the tabernacle and genuflected as he turned the key and unlocked the golden door. I felt my heart race, just as it had when I was about to kiss Wendy for the very first time. I realized that I had fallen so much in love with God—again!

Monsignor held the small white Host. "My brother Michael, this is the Lamb of God who takes away the sin of the world. Happy are those who have been called to receive Him."

"Lord, only say the word, and I shall be healed."

"My brother, receive the Body of Christ."

"Amen."

A week later I received Holy Communion with my wife and my son at his First Holy Communion, from the hands of Uncle Jerry.

I had one more thing to do; ironically, it was on May 16, the day that I was ordained a priest. I penned a handwritten letter to Pope Benedict XVI that was to be included in my petition. It read:

> *Most Holy Father, humbly prostrate at your feet...I request of you a dispensation from the obligations connected with my ordination to priesthood, including celibacy, and a return to the lay state. My petition and the favor that I request are made in a spirit of sincere penitence and with great humility...I seek this dispensation and favor for the salvation of my soul...I did not bring honor or respect to the ministry of priesthood...It has been through this grace–filled process of seeking dispensation*

that I continue to realize the gravity of my sinful ways...I seek
this dispensation and to return because I have a responsibil-
ity to provide for the spiritual welfare of my family. I cannot
achieve this continuing to live in the current state. Following
a pilgrimage my family made to Medjugorje, in thanksgiving to
God for my wife's healing from cancer, my wife and I felt called
to become reconciled with the Roman Catholic Church. Most
Holy Father, I make this request in my own hand.

—Michael

I worked at the funeral home for another month before we decided I should quit. I did not leave because of the job, but rather to spend time with Isaac on his summer break, a moment in 'Dadhood' I knew would not return.

During those summer days together, we worked in the yard, ate peanut butter and jelly sandwiches under the maple tree, read books to each other, and fished in a nearby pond. We climbed trees, played scenes from Star Wars, road mountain bikes through the trails of a nearby camp. And we laughed a lot. We ended every day praying the rosary with Wendy and Pappy. Isaac would fall asleep on the nearby couch, while Wendy and I prayed and pondered the next step in our lives.

Curiously, the recurring dream I had suffered for so long the vision of the hideous demonic creature hovering over me ended after our decision to return to the Catholic Church. The dreams actually ended when I sent the letter to the pope. To me the timing was more than coincidence.

Even though our house never sold, the financial burdens we envisioned never really materialized. Somehow, there was always just enough money to pay the bills. We came to believe that God wanted us to stay where we were—at least for the moment. Even though we had no clue where we would end up, or what my work would be, or just how poor we would eventually become—summer just seemed to get better and better. Everything became a celebration. True freedom in the soul can do that.

By the end of summer, all the paperwork was ready to be sent to Rome. The final step was for Wendy and me to make a solemn profession of the Faith in front of Bishop Hoffman.

We both finished reciting the Creed in unison: "…I believe in the Holy Spirit, one holy Catholic and Apostolic Church, the Communion of Saints, the forgiveness of sins, the resurrection of the body, and life everlasting. Amen."

"Amen," Bishop Hoffman offered. "Now where is that Isaac?"

"Hopefully he's with his Pappy," Wendy said, smiling. "The two of them were walking around the chapel."

"Well, let's see," the bishop said. He walked into an adjourning room. "I don't have anything that would be a good gift for an eight-year-old boy. He kept talking as he was looking around. "Ahh… maybe this!" He reappeared holding a small carved wooden box. "This is a rosary from the Holy Land and a little box to keep it in. Do you think he'd like something like this?"

"Bishop, that's perfect for him," Wendy said. "He collects rosaries!"

I stood in the hallway and watched as Isaac thanked the bishop. Straight ahead through the glass doors of the chapel, I noticed the tabernacle way up in the front of the sanctuary. A red candle burned brightly beside it.

Autumn came and went, and even though I knew it was too soon, I still hoped for a quick response from the Vatican. Wendy and I could not get married until I was cleared. Out of respect for the Church, God and each other, we had committed to living as celibates until we could be married in the Church. Talk about irony—an ex–celibate now living as a celibate until he is released from celibacy!

Advent and its inherent themes of anticipation and reconciliation took on a much deeper meaning to me. Christmas week came and passed; still no word. How could I expect anything? It had barely been one year since I was an Episcopal priest.

I was in the kitchen when the telephone rang. "Hello?"

"Merry Christmas to you, Michael! This is Bishop Hoffman."

"Well, thank you...Merry Christmas to you, Bishop."

"You know, it still is the Christmas season, so it is a great time to receive the news of this gift! I was out of town and just returned late today, and on my desk was your signed release from Pope Benedict—praise God!"

I couldn't feel my legs.

By now, Wendy, Isaac and Pappy were standing nearby in the kitchen—like some spiritual force had drawn them there. It was a dose of grace, which lit up the darkness of winter in our kitchen.

"Michael, all we need to do now is have you sign this document. Then we can set a time to have your marriage blessed and validated. Are you free to come in at all this week?"

"Sure, how about tomorrow afternoon? Wendy finishes work early and I want her to be there with me."

In the Roman calendar it was the Feast of the Conversion of St. Paul. Wendy and I sat at the table with Bishop Hoffman and the Vicar General. The bishop slid the documents from the Vatican across the table to me. It read: "His Holiness, Pope Benedict XVI, on the 12 day of December 2006, having received and considered the report from the Congregation for the Clergy, gives his consent to the requests in accord with the following conditions…"

Immediately, I noticed the date; the Pope received, considered and gave his consent to my petition on the Feast Day of Our Lady of Guadalupe. I didn't care if there were conditions or stipulations—the date said it all.

We sat at the table as the bishop read the entire document aloud to us. Outside a thick blanket of snow was covering the earth. Everything seemed to be coming together in slow motion, as though all of the parts of my life were finally being connected.

"Now Michael," the bishop said, pointing to where I needed to sign, "This does not mean that by being ordained you made a mistake. It's just that life does not always go the way we intended it. You have a beautiful wife and a wonderful little boy. God and the Blessed Mother have taken care of all of you. I know that it was a sacrifice to return. You all did the right thing."

I felt instant relief as though a cool glass of water had quenched a 10–year thirst. The bishop tapped the papers, placed them in a file and then asked, "Have the two of you given any thought as to when or whom you would want to do your marriage?"

In an unplanned unison, Wendy and I both said, "Bishop, we would like you to marry us."

"I would be honored," the bishop said. He went into his office and came out with his calendar. Flipping the pages he said, "Let's see…"

On a cold, blustery January night, in a side chapel of a church called Our Lady of Peace—her title at Medjugorje—the candles were lit and the altar was readied. Isaac read the scripture perfectly. Wendy and I stood before the altar and the crucifix, following the bishop's homily. Around us were a couple of friends and brother priests, everyone somehow connected through the Blessed Virgin Mary.

On the altar of my heart, I laid my promises to my wife, promises of eternal union: *I take you, Wendy, to be my wife. I promise to be true to you in good times and in bad, in sickness and in health. I will love you and honor you all the days of my life.*

At that moment, I heard God speaking those same words to me.

I was no longer a Lost Shepherd.

ABOUT THE AUTHOR

From an early age, Michael Ripple felt called to one day become an ordained Roman Catholic priest. He fulfilled that calling at a young age, only to discover in the following years of service disillusionment and disenchantment with the church he pledged to serve. Five years after ordination, Michael Ripple left the priesthood, married and began a new life as a husband and a father.

After leaving the Catholic Church, Michael worked as a therapist for a short time. Longing for a stable faith life, he and his young family joined the Episcopal Church. Still feeling the call to serve God in ministry, Michael became an Episcopal priest and rector. Life as a married priest with a loving wife and beautiful son seemed to be the solution of finally achieving his childhood dream of serving God in ministry; yet, something was missing.

In 2005, with his wife Wendy and six–year–old son Isaac, Michael made a pilgrimage to Medjugorje in thanksgiving for Wendy's healing from cancer. While in Medjugorje, he strongly felt called by the Blessed Virgin Mary to reconcile with the Roman Catholic Church—a church from which he had been ex–communicated. In a near–miraculous short span of time, Michael and his family returned to the Catholic Church.

Michael is currently involved in parish faith formation for youth, with an emphasis on sharing the messages of Medjugorje. He and his wife Wendy lead pilgrimages to Medjugorje and Michael gives talks and retreats on a variety of spiritual topics. He reaches a broad audience because of the wealth of his experiences as a husband, father, priest, therapist, protestant minister and even ex–communicant.

At home, Michael enjoys family adventures, bicycling, cooking, fly fishing, building projects, and music composition. He lives with his lovely wife and son, father, brother, and several unruly dogs.

A Lost Shepherd, is a fascinating memoir of Michael's personal journey from faith, to sin, to redemption.

NOTES